REREADING GALATIANS
from THE PERSPECTIVE
of PAUL'S GOSPEL

REREADING GALATIANS
from THE PERSPECTIVE
of PAUL'S GOSPEL

A Literary and Theological Commentary

Yung Suk Kim

CASCADE *Books* • Eugene, Oregon

REREADING GALATIANS FROM THE PERSPECTIVE OF PAUL'S GOSPEL
A Literary and Theological Commentary

Cascade Books
An Imprint of Wipf and Stock Publishers
199 W. 8th Ave., Suite 3
Eugene, OR 97401

www.wipfandstock.com

PAPERBACK ISBN: 978-1-5326-9112-6
HARDCOVER ISBN: 978-1-5326-9113-3
EBOOK ISBN: 978-1-5326-9114-0

Cataloguing-in-Publication data:

Names: Kim, Yung Suk.

Title: Rereading Galatians from the perspective of Paul's gospel : a literary and theological commentary / Yung Suk Kim.

Description: Eugene, OR: Cascade Books, 2019 | Includes bibliographical references.

Identifiers: ISBN 978-1-5326-9112-6 (paperback) | ISBN 978-1-5326-9113-3 (hardcover) | ISBN 978-1-5326-9114-0 (ebook)

Subjects: LCSH: Bible—Galatians—Commentaries | Bible—Galatians—Criticism, interpretation, etc.

Classification: BS2685.53 K435 2019 (paperback) | BS2685.53 (ebook)

Manufactured in the U.S.A.   04/18/19

Contents

Acknowledgments | vii

Introduction | 1

SECTION I
1:1–10. The Letter's Opening | 14
1:1–5 Greeting | 15
1:6–10 Confusion about the Gospel | 22

SECTION II
1:11–24. The Origin of the Gospel | 29
1:11–17 God's Revelation of Jesus Christ | 29
1:18–24 Independent of Jerusalem Churches | 32

SECTION III
2:1–21. The Clarification of the Gospel | 34
2:1–10 The Gospel at the Council of Jerusalem | 34
2:11–14 The Incident at Antioch | 37
2:15–21 Justification by Christ Jesus's Faithfulness | 41

SECTION IV
3:1–29. The Root of the Gospel | 53
A 3:1–5 Confusion in the Church Due to the Lack of Faith | 55
B 3:6–12 The Gospel through Abraham's Faith | 59
C 3:13–16 Receiving the Promise of the Spirit through Christ | 61
D 3:17–18 The Gospel Rooted in God's Promise | 64
C' 3:19–21 God's Promises Do Not Depend on the Law | 65
B' 3:22–25 The Gospel through Jesus Christ's Faithfulness | 66
A' 3:26–29 A New Vision of the Community in Christ | 69

SECTION V
4:1–31. The Advantage of the Gospel | 73

A 4:1–7 God's Assurance of His Children | 74
B 4:8–11 How Can You Turn Back Again to the Elemental Spirits? | 77
B′ 4:12–20 Return to the Gospel | 78
A′ 4:21–31 "We Are Children, Not of the Slave But of the Free Woman" | 80

SECTION VI
5:1—6:10. The Mandate of the Gospel | 84

5:1–15 "Stand Firm in Christ; Do Not Submit Again to a Yoke of Slavery" | 85
5:16–26 "Live by the Spirit" | 89
6:1–10 "Fulfill the Law of Christ" | 91

SECTION VII
6:11–18. The Letter's Conclusion | 93

Bibliography | 97

Acknowledgments

I WOULD LIKE TO thank the faculty, staff, and students at the Samuel DeWitt Proctor School of Theology, Virginia Union University, for their unwavering support for my teaching and research. I would like to give my special thanks to my dear colleague Robert Wafawanaka, Associate Professor of Hebrew Bible, who has read the entire manuscript and has given me helpful feedback. In school or outside, we have had pleasant conversations about many topics of teaching and research. I cannot miss thanking L. L. Welborn, Professor of New Testament at Fordham University, who is my mentor, colleague, and friend. He has never said no to my scholarly endeavor, always encouraging me to do more. I cheer with him. I also need to mention Ekaputra Tupamahu, Assistant Professor of New Testament at Portland Seminary, George Fox University. He has been supportive of me as a scholar and friend. Dale Martin, Emeritus Professor of Religious Studies at Yale University, took pains to read the entire manuscript and provided helpful critical comments and suggestions for editing. His kindness and scholarly rigor will not be forgotten for a long time. Lastly, I must thank my family: my wife, Yongjeong, and my beautiful daughters, Hyerim, HyeKyung, and HyeIn. They are my joy and love.

Introduction

SCHOLARS OFTEN THINK THAT Romans is a more mature theological letter than Galatians.[1] But this view needs to be tested since Paul's core thinking about the gospel remains similar between these two letters. While Galatians' context is different from Romans, it also contains the gist of the gospel that all people can become children of God through faith (Gal 4:1–7; Rom 3:21–26; 5:1–21).[2] As Paul's gospel begins with "the good news about or from God" in Romans (Rom 1:1), in Galatian as well, his gospel begins with God's revelation of his Son (Gal 1:15–16). He argues that the gospel is rooted in the promise of God (Gal 3:17–21).[3] Furthermore, he says in Gal

---

1. For example, see Hans Hübner, *Law in Paul's Thought*, 15–86. According to him, in Galatians, Paul sees the law very negatively, and Christ ends it. But in Romans, he thinks "Christ is the end of the misuse of the Law" (138). But in a closer analysis of Galatians, the law is not rejected because it is the law. The problem is the *misuse* of the law or the *absolutizing* tendency of certain laws or works of the law, such as circumcision or food laws.

2. The only big difference between Romans and Galatians is about the context of each letter. Romans was written to the house churches in Rome, which Paul did not found, to garner support from them for a planned trip to Spain for his final mission. Even though he did not visit Rome or found churches there, he had some concerns about them. For example, some gentile Christians were antinomian and rejected Jewish laws or place. So Paul clarifies his gospel of faith to make clear that it does not reject Israel or Jewish laws. Galatians was written to the churches in Galatia to deal with issues of circumcision and the works of the law. Here also, Paul makes clear that the gospel of faith does not reject the law per se.

3. This alternative reading of Galatians does not emphasize Paul's autobiographical experience. While his experience of the Spirit or a revelation from God is important to him, that is not the root of his gospel. This is where my reading of Galatians is different from Hans Betz, who wrote a major rhetorical commentary on Galatians. He analyzes Galatians as an apologetic letter, using ancient rhetoric. With the rhetorical analysis, his conclusion about the gospel is the same as that of Luther, who reads Paul as a champion of faith *over against* the law. He follows the traditional interpretation of Luther emphasizing individual justification by faith. But my alternative reading does not employ ancient

3:8: "And the scripture, foreseeing that God would justify the gentiles by faith, declared the gospel beforehand to Abraham, saying, 'All the gentiles shall be blessed in you.'" In Rom 1:16, the gospel is said to be "the power of God for salvation to everyone who has faith, to the Jew first and also to the Greek." Likewise, in Gal 3:26–29, Paul talks about the power of the gospel:

> 26 For in Christ Jesus you are all children of God through faith. 27 As many of you as were baptized into Christ have clothed your-selves with Christ. 28 There is no longer Jew or Greek, there is no longer slave or free, there is no longer male and female; for all of you are one in Christ Jesus. 29 And if you belong to Christ, then you are Abraham's offspring, heirs according to the promise.[4]

In both Romans and Galatians, the gospel of God concerns Jesus, Son of God. Romans 1:3–4 reads: "the gospel concerning his Son, who was de-scended from David according to the flesh and was declared to be Son of God with power according to the spirit of holiness by resurrection from the dead, Jesus Christ our Lord." Jesus was affirmed for the work of God he performed, for he was faithful to God, as Rom 3:22 indicates: "God's righ-teousness through *the faithfulness of Jesus Christ* for all who believe." In this book, *pistis christou* phrases in Rom 3:22 and Gal 2:16 are taken as a sub-jective genitive ("the faithfulness *of* Christ" rather than "faith *in* Christ"). Paul emphasizes the primacy of Christ's faithfulness that revealed God's righteousness, which is primarily understood as God's love and justice.

In both Romans and Galatians, faith means trusting God, following Jesus, and participating in his faithfulness (Rom 3:21–26; Gal 2:16). All those who follow Jesus and his faithfulness are justified by God and join the people of God. This is the good news Paul is eager to share with the gentiles. In Galatians, Paul elaborates this gospel of faith to the Galatians. When they follow Jesus and his faithfulness, they stay free in Christ and belong to God (Rom 8:1; Gal 5:13).[5] Here freedom in Christ does not mean one

---

rhetoric and focuses on the internal logic of the theme of the gospel. See Hans Betz, *Galatians*.

4. All translations of the NT are from the New Revised Standard Version except when otherwise noted. However, note the following two general modifications: (a) I have fol-lowed the SBL-recommended "gentile" rather than the NRSV's "Gentile." (b) I modify the NRSV's objective genitive translation of *pistis christou* for a subjective genitive transla-tion. Thus, for instance, in Gal 2:20 I change the NRSV's "I live by faith in the Son of God" to "I live by the faith of the Son of God."

5. For more about freedom in the New Testament, see Yung Suk Kim, *Preaching the New Testament Again*, 37–73.

is free to do anything, but it means one belongs to God through faith, the faith that Jesus has shown. That is, those who follow Jesus and participate in his faithfulness may live a life of freedom away from "the present evil age" (Gal 1:4; cf. Rom 8:1–2).

Likewise, justification means a good right relationship with God, which is made possible through the way of Jesus or his faithfulness (Rom 3:22; Gal 2:16). For Paul, justification is, mainly, a concept of relational language while a forensic concept is not completely ruled out. To buttress this point, Paul quotes from Hab 2:4 and writes in Rom 1:17: "The righteous one will live by faith." This implies that justification is not made once and for all. In Rom 3:26, he nails justification language by relating to Christ's faith: "God justifies the one who has *the faith of Jesus.*" The Greek genitive case in this verse (*pisteōs Iesou*) can be the subjective genitive ("faith *of* Jesus") rather than the objective genitive ("faith *in* Jesus"). This idea of the subjective genitive is found both in Rom 3:22 and Gal 2:16 (*pisteōs Iesou Christou*). That is, justification is made possible through one's participation in Christ's faithfulness.[6] In Gal 2:16, Paul's point is one's justification is not possible by the works of the law, such as circumcision or specific works of the law, but through Christ Jesus's faithfulness. The above common understanding between Romans and Galatians is important because the former may be useful for interpreting the latter.

Nevertheless, Galatians is distinguished from Romans and other letters of Paul, and the penetrating, troubling issue is circumcision. That is, Christian Jews, whether they were local or came from the Jerusalem church, persuaded gentile Christians to be circumcised because faith alone was not enough.[7] Their teaching is that gentile Christians should honor

---

6. See Yung Suk Kim, *A Theological Introduction to Paul's Letters*, 63–82.

7. The majority view of Paul's so-called opponents in Galatia is that they are Christian Jews who insist on circumcision in addition to faith. While Paul's opponents are primarily Christian Jews, they may include "the righteous gentiles" who accepted Jewish law and practices and influenced the churches of Galatia, as Mark Nanos argues. Nanos, *The Irony of Galatians*, 193–200. A similar argument is also found in Theissen, *Paul and the Gentile Problem*, 19–102. While Theissen argues that Paul's polemics are directed only against the gentiles who insist on circumcision, I see his polemics can be directed to Christian Jews who believed that circumcision was necessary to the gentiles. Their scriptural base is Gen 17:14: "Any uncircumcised male who is not circumcised in the flesh of his foreskin shall be cut off from his people; he has broken my covenant." That is, while the gentiles may be included as children of God through Christ Jesus, they still need circumcision because it is God's law. That said, it is possible that some gentile Christians accepted this view and influenced their fellow Christians. Another indication that Paul's primary polemics are directed to Christian Jews is "a different gospel" (Gal

Jewish tradition and accept Jewish laws such as circumcision or dietary laws. Some members of the Galatian *ekklēsia* followed this teaching and were confused about Paul's gospel, which places priority on faith. In fact, the Christian Jews' demand as such does not seem strange or baseless as Gen 17:14 clearly puts the condition for staying in a covenantal community: "Any uncircumcised male who is not circumcised in the flesh of his foreskin shall be cut off from his people; he has broken my covenant." For Christian Jews, circumcision is more than a matter of the law; it is a sign of the covenant between God and his people. Therefore, in order to belong to this covenantal community, gentile Christians must undergo circumcision.

But Paul does not begin with circumcision in Gen 17. He begins with God's call of Abraham in Gen 12, arguing that Abraham's faith came *before* the introduction of circumcision. That is, Abraham's *faith* is the basis of the covenantal community. Therefore, what is urgent and necessary to the gentile Christians is not circumcision or any works of the law, such as circumcision or dietary regulations, but faith—just like the faith of Abraham and of Jesus—which Paul explains in detail throughout the letter.[8] Paul emphasizes this kind of faith in Gal 5:6: "For in Christ Jesus neither circumcision nor uncircumcision counts for anything; the only thing that counts is faith working through love." Christians' faith means the *faithfulness* of Christians. It is not simply believing something or accepting Jesus's salvific work but following his faith. As such, it is not separated from works.

While not thinking of the two different gospels—one for Jews and one for the gentiles, Paul acknowledges that the one gospel applies to Jews differently, as they may keep the law. This idea is seen in the phrase "a different gospel" (*eis heteron euangelion*, 1:6), which hints at that idea. Here "different" conveys the idea that this Jewish version of the one gospel is not wrong but different. This particular version of the gospel may work well with Jews. That is, for Jews, faith may go side by side with Jewish laws and culture. Likewise, for them, faith and circumcision may work together. But even in this Jewish version of the gospel, the law does not take priority. As long as faith takes priority over other things, their gospel is not wrong, but different.

1:6–7), which implies a different version of the gospel, that is for Jews, who may keep the Jewish law and practices.

8. For more about Christians' faithfulness, see Kim, *Preaching the New Testament Again*, 23–27.

But when it comes to the gentile Christians, the issue is different because they are not familiar with Jewish culture or tradition, especially circumcision or dietary laws. To them, Jewish culture and faith do not go side by side. So those "Jewish" things are not indispensable to the gospel to the gentiles because the essential thing is faith. In other words, Jewish laws or customs should not be given priority over the gospel. Moreover, Paul is concerned that if those things are imposed onto them, there will be no freedom in Christ (Gal 5:1). Paul does not want the freedom of the Galatians to be compromised due to "the works of the law" such as circumcision or dietary laws or anything else.[9] So in his gospel for the gentiles, which is no less Jewish a gospel (i.e., no less true to Israel's scriptures), he does not attach any "strings" to it. He is against law-centered or culture-driven religiosity. Instead, he elevates the "faith working through love," as he says in 5:6: "For in Christ Jesus neither circumcision nor uncircumcision counts for anything; the only thing that counts is faith working through love." Obviously, even here, Paul does not reject the law itself, as he says clearly that the law is summed up in a single commandment (Gal 5:14). Faith does not replace the law; his point is the law must be interpreted through faith and love. The law without faith may be void or aimless.

Yet Paul disavows "another gospel," as he says in 1:17: "not that there is another gospel" (*ho ouk estin allo*). While there may be different implications of the gospel for Jews, the gospel is one and the same for both Jews and gentiles. Even if there may be a cosmetic change about the gospel, the essence of the gospel remains the same, as faith is one and the same for all, as he says in Rom 3:30: "since God is one; and he will justify the circumcised on the ground of faith and the uncircumcised through that same faith." While the Jewish version of the gospel seems a bit different, it does not mean there are two different gospels or two different ways of justification or salvation—one for the Jews and one for the gentiles.[10] The two-paths theory is often postulated by some scholars. But throughout his letters, Paul never thinks the gospel he proclaims is only for gentiles and that Jews do not need it since they are already children of God. Rather, although his focus is on gentiles, he claims that the gospel is for both Jews and gentiles. For example, see Rom 1:16: "For I am not ashamed of the gospel; it is the

---

9. Dunn, *The Epistle to the Galatians*, 21–348.

10. See my book review, Kim, Review of Pamela Eisenbaum, *Paul Was Not a Christian*. Those who argue for a two-paths theory are found in the following works, to name a few: Gager, *Reinventing Paul*; Eisenbaum, *Paul Was Not a Christian*; Fredriksen, *Paul: The Pagans' Apostle*.

power of God for salvation to everyone who has faith, to the Jew first and also to the Greek."

ALTERNATIVE READING OF GALATIANS

Traditionally, Galatians, as well as Romans, has been read as advocating the doctrine of "justification by faith" from a forensic salvation perspective. In this doctrine, justification is understood as an individual justification once and for all. That is, sinners in a court are declared righteous by the judge, who is God, because of Jesus's vicarious death. In this view, Jesus completed the salvific work by dying on the cross on behalf of sinners, and sins were dealt with by his death. He delivered sinners from the grip of the devil by paying the ransom (ransom theory). He was punished and died instead of sinners (penal-substitution theory). His sacrifice was a propitiation to allay God's wrath (propitiation theory). His death was a cost needing to restore a broken relationship between God and humanity (expiation theory). His sinless sacrifice was a perfect means to satisfy God's moral demand for humanity (satisfaction theory). In all the above atonement theories, Jesus's death is necessary to deal with sins, and what believers need is faith in him. If they believe and accept his salvific death, their sins are cleansed or dealt with.

Likewise, interpreters have read Gal 2:16 and 3:22 in view of the doctrine of "justification by faith" and translated *pistis christou* as an objective genitive: "faith in Christ." Most English Bibles, including the New Revised Standard Version (NRSV) and New International Version (NIV), have this objective genitive translation. Galatians 2:16 in the NRSV is as follows: "yet we know that a person is justified not by the works of the law but through *faith in Jesus Christ*. And we have come to believe in Christ Jesus, so that we might be justified by *faith in Christ*, and not by doing the works of the law because no one will be justified by the works of the law." Similarly, Gal 3:22 in the NRSV is as follows: "But the scripture has imprisoned all things under the power of sin so that what was promised through *faith in Jesus Christ* might be given to those who believe." This translation serves the doctrine of "individual justification by faith" in that Christ completed the salvific work.[11]

---

11. This translation of "faith in Christ" reflects both the old perspective on Paul and E. P. Sanders's view of the move "from solution to plight." In the former, the law is considered an impossible means of salvation. But even in the latter, while the law is itself

But the Common English Bible (CEB) translates *pistis christou* in both these verses as a subjective genitive case: "through the faithfulness of Jesus Christ." This translation makes better sense than the NRSV because, as we will see throughout this book, one can be set right with God through Christ's faithfulness (cf. Rom 3:22, 26). That is, when one shares Jesus's faithfulness, one is set right with God. On this meaning, the concept of "justification" has to do with one's relationship with God. This relationship needs one's faith and commitment. In Genesis 12, when Abraham was called by God, he responded to God with faith and walked his faith journey through his entire life. Even though he was not perfect, going through the ups and downs, he did not give up on his faith. In this sense, the righteous person will live by faith (Hab 2:4). Jesus also showed his faithfulness to God, disclosing God's righteousness at all costs (cf. Rom 3:22). In other words, he did not come simply to die instead of sinners or to cleanse sins.

Therefore, we need an alternative reading of Galatians that emphasizes the faithfulness of Jesus, which goes back to God's faithfulness. Indeed, faith is the most prevalent theme in the Hebrew Bible as well as in the New Testament. God is the one who is faithful, loving, and righteous. God is *chesed* ("loving kindness"), which appears more than 200 times, and God is also "righteousness, justice, or vindication" (*tsedāqâ*), which appears more than 150 times in the Bible. Abraham's call is based on God's faithfulness. Abraham was also faithful to God, enduring in his faith journey. Many prophets and God's agents tried to live faithfully. Jesus as the Son of God was faithful and demonstrated God's righteousness. That is, Jesus lived faithfully to reveal that God is righteousness, justice, peace, and love. Because he did not spare his life doing his job, he was crucified, but God raised him from the dead and makes him live (cf. 2 Cor 13:4). Christ became the Lord of all and was exalted and seated at the right hand of God. Obviously, for Paul, Jesus is more than Abraham or any person of faith in

---

good, it cannot be the means of salvation because of Christ. In Sanders's view, because Paul believed that Christ was the Messiah and solved matters of salvation, the law must be wrong ("plight"). But Frank Thielman presents an alternative perspective of a "from plight to solution" pattern. He argues that for Paul, the law was a plight not because of its impossible means, but because of people (Jews) disobeying the law of God. This problem was solved through God's intervention in the world and in Christ. While Thielman's view of the law makes better sense than Sanders's, both of them still translate *pistis christou* as "faith in Christ." This is a problem because Paul's emphasis on Christ is his faithfulness through which God's righteousness has been manifested (Rom 3:22). Throughout this book, we will see the importance of Christ's faith. See Thielman, *From Plight to Solution*. Sanders, *Paul and Palestinian Judaism*; *Paul, the Law, and the Jewish People*.

history. Through Jesus Christ, the Son of God, redemption is possible (cf. Rom 3:24). Here redemption means liberation, a new life in the Spirit and away from a sinful life ruled by sinful passions.[12]

As Christ was faithful to God, his followers have to be faithful to God, following the example of Jesus's faithfulness. Jesus's spirit becomes available for his followers, as Paul says in Gal 4:6: "And because you are children, God has sent the spirit of his Son into our hearts, crying, 'Abba! Father!'" In 1 Cor 15:45, he also says Christ became "a life-giving spirit," which means he continues to work for his followers.

Christian faith is not merely to accept Jesus or his salvific death as such, but to participate in his faithfulness. If so, Gal 2:16 is understood differently. One can live righteously through Christ's faithfulness. A new life in the Spirit is not merely possible by faith in Christ but through his faithfulness. To be faithful to God, one must know Jesus's faithfulness to God. Thus, in Gal 2:20, Paul confesses the importance of Christ's faithfulness in his life. He says Christ lives in him and he wants to live in (or by) "the faithfulness of the Son of God, who loved me and gave himself to me." Here again, we interpret *pistis christou* as a subjective genitive, which makes better sense than the objective genitive. Paul's point is not that he wants to live "by faith in Christ" but that he wants to live "by Christ's faithfulness" because Christ is everything to him. Thus, he says: "and it is no longer I who live, but it is Christ who lives in me. And the life I now live in the flesh I live by *the faithfulness of the Son of God*, who loved me and gave himself for me." Paul says Christ lives in him, and therefore, he is informed and shaped by Christ and decides to live by the faith of Jesus who loved him and gave himself for him. How can we say that Paul does not talk about Christ's faithfulness?[13]

In the above alternative reading of Galatians, there are three dimensions of Paul's gospel: God as the *source* of the gospel; Christ Jesus as the *proclaimer and exemplifier* of the gospel; the followers of Jesus as *participants* of the gospel. Paul received a revelation from God (1:15–16). The content of that revelation is about Jesus, who revealed God's righteousness through faith. This is the gospel of Christ (1:9). The followers of Jesus are those who live by his faithfulness (2:16–21). It is important to see all these aspects in the gospel. Traditionally, the gospel is easily identified with a

---

12. About the role of the Spirit in Paul's Letters, see Fee, *God's Empowering Presence*, 839.

13. See Smith and Kim, *Toward Decentering the New Testament*, 246–52.

"gospel message" of which the content is Christ's vicarious death. But in Galatians as well as in Romans, the gospel involves all these three dimensions.

In this alternative reading of Galatians, it must be noted that Paul's gospel is not law-free in the sense of the old perspective on Paul, but it is strings-free.[14] Namely, specific rules or works of the law such as circumcision or dietary laws are not required for gentile Christians because what God wants is faithfulness. The law is not outdated or replaced by faith. Rather, it is summed up in a single commandment, "You shall love your neighbor as yourself" (Gal 5:14). Also, in this reading, the gospel is one and the same for both Jews and gentiles. The only difference is Jews may keep their religious traditions while staying in Christ. That is what "a different gospel" means and it may work with them. But fundamentally, the gospel is one for God is one and the same. In this alternative reading, we also see Christ's faithfulness and its importance to Christians. This means Jesus's death is not *in itself* important, as if he came to die for sinners. He died for sinners but the cause and meaning of his death go beyond the traditional atonement theories. His death must be understood as a moral sacrifice that he was willing to die to demonstrate God's righteousness.

Lastly, in this alternative reading of Galatians, I argue that Paul's theological thinking has not changed much over time. In other words, his view of the gospel, faith, justification, sin, or freedom is consistent in Galatians and Romans. Therefore, Romans will help us interpret Galatians and vice versa. Some think that Paul has a harsh view of the law in Galatians and tones it down in Romans. Certainly, his rhetoric in Galatians shows such a negative view of the law as he was upset with the Galatians. Even though his view of the law in Romans is smoother than Galatians, his actual views of the law between these two letters did not change. That is, what is opposed in both these letters is not the law *per se* but the law *without faith or Christ*.

---

14. Paul's position on the law is complex. But one thing is clear in that he does not reject the law per se. The law is summed up in a single commandment (Gal 5:14). He never says in Galatians the law is an impossible means of justification or salvation. Even in Gal 2:16, what is opposed is between "the works of the law" and "faith of Christ." That is, one may be justified by God when one lives by faith, the faithfulness of Jesus. The point is the priority of faith; otherwise, Jewish laws may be kept as long as they are interpreted through faith and love, as he implies it in Gal 5:6. Personally, Paul as a Jew may have kept Jewish laws and customs, but he insists *gentiles* do not need circumcision. At the same time, he thinks gentile Christians must honor and keep the spirit of the law as much as they can. See Fredriksen, "Why Should a 'Law-Free' Mission Mean a 'Law-Free' Apostle?" 637–50.

GOSPEL (GOOD NEWS) AND PAUL'S LETTERS

"Gospel" or "good news" comes from the Greek *euangelion*, which refers to kinds of good news in the Greco-Roman world. From the emperor's perspective, the good news is the victory of war or his birthday celebration. But from the perspective of the oppressed, the good news is their liberation from oppressors. Good news is also found in the Hebrew Bible. For example, it is a message of hope to Jewish exiles in Babylon. Classical prophets delivered God's good news to his people, asking for their change of mind toward God. The Synoptic Gospels also contain the good news about the kingdom of God that Jesus proclaimed. Jesus proclaims the good news that is markedly different from the emperor's good news. He teaches God must rule the world with justice, love, and peace, advocates for the oppressed, and challenges the status quo of society. He cures the sick and feeds the hungry, encouraging people not to give up hope in God and to expect a better world to come now and in the future. All he does in the gospel stories relates to the good news about or from God. In fact, Jesus's initial sermon is about God's good news, as in Mark 1:14–15: "Now after John was arrested, Jesus came to Galilee, proclaiming the good news of God, and saying, 'The time is fulfilled, and the kingdom of God has come near; repent, and believe in the good news.'" Now is the time of fulfilling God's good news in the world. It is now that people must hear the good news of God and experience a new life. And in this time now, the kingdom of God (*basileia thou*), which means God's reign or rule, has come near (the perfect tense). There are tensions between God's good news and the emperor's good news. Since God's rule came to the world, what is required is repentance (*metanoia*) of people. Here the Greek word for "repent" is *metanoeō*, which means a change of mind. Jesus does not simply ask for a penitential prayer or confession of sins. People have to accept the rule of God by changing their mind and seeking God's will. Likewise, rulers have to change their mind and seek God's will. This good news is not about Jesus but about God who rules the world with justice and peace. Jesus asks people "to believe in the good news." In a world where no real good news is directed to the oppressed and the poor, the good news is a new life full of love and justice.

The main theme in the Gospel of John is also the good news of God that Jesus brings to the world. Though there is no word of the "gospel" in that gospel, there is good news of God that Jesus delivers and lives out. For example, Jesus heals the sick and opens the eyes of a blind man (John 9).

He also feeds the hungry and talks about the way people have to follow God (John 6:1–14). He showed the way of truth and exemplified God's love (John 14). He says "I am the way, and the truth, and the life" (John 14:6), not because he is God but he incarnates God in his life. He also talks about the life informed by the Spirit when Nicodemus visits him (John 3:1–21). A new birth must be spiritual and it must be based on the Spirit of God. Even though the Fourth Gospel does not have parables, it has teachings about the kingdom of God in different ways, e.g., the story of Nicodemus. If the kingdom of God means God's realm or rule, John's Gospel is also full of implications and teachings about it. Jesus is sent by God to do the work of God, which is none other than providing life and light. He taught the word (*logos*) of God and embodied it.

Paul's undisputed letters chronologically precede the four Gospels and contain both the good news of God that Jesus brings to the world and the good news of Christ Jesus, which is good news about him and good news that he proclaimed. Since the letter is a different genre, Paul's letters do not include Jesus's birth stories or specific works of Jesus as in the Gospels. However, he talks about the significance of Jesus's work in relation to God and the world. For example, he emphasizes Christ's faithfulness, which revealed God's righteousness. Because of Christ's faithfulness, those who follow him may live a new life of freedom in Christ. In other words, Paul's undisputed letters are full of the good news of God and the good news of Christ. In Rom 1:1, he says he was called "apostle" and set apart for "the gospel of God." His mission is to proclaim the good news of God that Jesus brought to the world. The followers of Jesus "have received grace and apostleship" through Jesus, the Son of God. Therefore, they have to proclaim the good news of God through Jesus. The way Paul honors and worships God is through proclaiming the gospel concerning his Son (Rom 1:9). God is the one who is served and worshipped, and his Son is the one who disclosed God's righteousness through faith. God is pleased with his Son because he brought the good news of God to the world through faith. Paul senses his call for the gospel of God through Jesus and thinks himself "to be a minister of Christ Jesus to the gentiles in the priestly service of the gospel of God, so that the offering of the gentiles may be acceptable, sanctified by the Holy Spirit" (Rom 15:16).

In Galatians too, the main theme is the gospel. See the outline below:

I. 1:1–10 The Letter's Opening
1:1–5   Greeting
1:6–10   Confusion about the gospel

II. 1:11–24 The Origin of the Gospel
1:11–17   God's revelation of Jesus Christ
1:18–24   Independent of Jerusalem churches

III. 2:1–21 The Clarification of the Gospel
2:1–10   The gospel at the Council of Jerusalem
2:11–14   The incident at Antioch
2:15–21   Justification by Christ Jesus's faithfulness

IV. 3:1–29 The Root of the Gospel
3:1–5   Confusion in the church due to the lack of faith
3:6–12   The gospel through Abraham's faith
3:13–16   Receiving the promise of the Spirit through Christ
3:17–18   The gospel rooted in God's promise
3:19–21   God's promises do not depend on the law
3:22–25   The gospel through Jesus Christ's faithfulness
3:26–29   A new union of a community in Christ

V. 4:1–31 The Advantage of the Gospel
4:1–7   God's assurance of his children
4:8–11   How can you turn back again to the elemental spirits?
4:12–20   Return to the gospel
4:21–31   "We are children, not of the slave but of the free woman"

VI. 5:1—6:10 The Mandate of the Gospel
5:1–15   "Stand firm in Christ; Do not submit again to a yoke of slavery"
5:16–26   "Live the Spirit"
6:1–10   "Fulfill the law of Christ"

VII. 6:11–18 The Letter's Conclusion

As seen above, the gospel is a common thread through which the whole letter is structured and understood.[15] After greeting (1:1–5), Paul

---

15. This book does not employ a rhetorical approach informed by ancient rhetorical theories. Hans Betz sees Galatians as the "apologetic letter" genre and analyzes the letter as follows: The prescript (1:1–5); The exordium (1:6–11); The narratio (1:12—2:14); The proposito (2:15–21); The probatio (3:1—4:31); The paraenesis (5:1—6:10); The postscript (6:11–18). In Betz's rhetorical analysis, the defensive thesis is 2:15–21 ("justification by

introduces the issue of the gospel (1:6–10). Then the origin of the gospel is discussed in 1:11–24. Then the gospel is clarified in relation to the Jewish tradition (2:1–21). After this, there is a section on the root of the gospel (3:1–29) where the gospel is built on the ground of God's promise to Abraham. After this, there are two more sections on the gospel: "the advantage of the gospel" (4:1–31) and "the mandate of the gospel" (5:1–6:10). The advantage of the gospel includes the assurance of the children of God. Lastly, the mandate of the gospel exhorts Galatians to live by the Spirit and fulfill the law of Christ. The letter ends with a conclusion (6:11–18).

Paul writes Galatians not to argue for "justification by faith" but to make explicit the gospel he proclaimed—the good news that all can become children of God through faith. This gospel originated in God, was proclaimed and exemplified by Jesus, and continues to be proclaimed by the followers of Jesus.

Thus far we have seen the consistent theme of the good news in the Gospels and Paul's undisputed letters. In the Gospels, the main character is Jesus who proclaimed the good news of God. Each gospel, depending on its historical context, portrays Jesus differently with a focus on different aspects of God's good news or God's rule.[16] Paul's letters are not a storybook, but they also contain the good news of God and the good news of Jesus. Paul is committed to proclaiming the gospel of God to the gentiles.

---

faith"). But Robert Hall and Joop Smit challenge Betz's reading and argue that Galatians has more to do with deliberative rhetoric. So Hall's division of the letter differs from Betz: Salutation/Exordium (1:1–5); Proposition (1:6–9); Proof (1:10–6:10): A) Narration (1:10–2:21); B) Further Headings (3:1–6:10); Epilogue (6:11–18). Smit's analysis of Paul's speech is as follows: Exordium (1:6–12); Narratio (1:13–2:21); Confirmatio (3:1–4:11); Conclusio, Part 1: Conquestio (4:12–20); Conclusio, Part 2: Enumeratio (4:21–5:6); Amplificatio (6:11–18). What we can know here is that application of ancient rhetorical theory to Galatians is helpful yet arbitrary. In reality, as Robert Hall argues, Paul may have all three types of rhetoric in his mind: judiciary (defense), deliberative, and epideictic. Paul certainly defends his apostleship (so apologetic letter). But he also makes an exhortation to the Galatians about the truth of the gospel (so deliberative letter). He also employs "the speech of praise and censure which is held at special occasions" (Smit, "The Letter of Paul to the Galatians," 43). Therefore, while rhetorical approach to Galatians may be helpful to understand Paul's motif of letter writing, we should not limit to just one analysis. This book analyzes Galatians as a letter with a focus on the theme of the gospel within the letter. With this approach, the letter is outlined and commented briefly. See Betz, "The Literary Composition and Function of Paul's Letter to the Galatians," 3–28; Berchman, "Galatians (1:1–5): Paul and Greco-Roman Rhetoric," 60–72; Hall, "The Rhetorical Outline for Galatians," 29–38; Smit, "The Letter of Paul to the Galatians," 39–59.

16. For example, Jesus states the purpose of his coming to the world differently in the Gospels: Mark 10:45; Matt 5:17; Luke 19:10; John 18:37.

SECTION I

1:1–10

The Letter's Opening

GALATIANS 1:1–10 IS THE letter's opening in which Paul emphasizes his independent apostleship, which is not based on any human commission or human authorities, but based on Jesus Christ and God. He then greets the Galatians, and introduces the topic of the letter, which is "the gospel." This gospel has to do with Jesus's work, as stated in Gal 1:4: "who gave himself for our sins to set us free from the present evil age, according to the will of our God and Father." This gospel is none other than "the gospel of Christ" (Gal 1:7), which means the good news that Jesus proclaimed and the good news about him, namely his faithfulness and sacrifice for people. His work of the good news is "according to the will of our God and Father, to whom be the glory forever and ever" (Gal 1:4b–5). This relationship between God and Jesus is important to his gospel. God is the one who "raised him [Jesus] from the dead" (Gal 1:1) and "to whom be the glory forever" (Gal 1:5). Jesus is the one who worked according to the will of God. He was crucified because of that, but God raised him from the dead. In this letter opening, Paul raises the issue of confusion or misunderstanding about the gospel due to "a different gospel" (Gal 1:6–10). He is astonished because "there are some who are confusing the Galatians and perverting the gospel of Christ" (Gal 1:7). He confronts those who proclaim a gospel contrary to the one he proclaimed (Gal 1:8).

1:1-5 GREETING

1 Paul an apostle, who is not sent from human authority or commissioned through human agency, but sent through Jesus Christ and God the Father, who raised him from the dead— 2 and all the fellow Christians who are with me, To the churches of Galatia: 3 Grace to you and peace from God our Father and the Lord Jesus Christ, 4 who gave himself for our sins to set us free from the present evil age, according to the will of our God and Father, 5 to whom be the glory forever and ever. Amen.

Each letter's beginning is important because it reflects Paul's concern and hints at the purpose of the writing. No two of his letter beginnings are the same. For example, in 1 Thess 1:1, he writes sender names without adding any modifiers to them: "Paul, Silvanus, and Timothy." This is maybe because there is no need to add more since the Thessalonian church is doing well. But in Phlm 1:1, he begins with "Paul, a prisoner of Christ Jesus." This is not only because he was imprisoned when he wrote Philemon but because he cares for Onesimus, a slave to Philemon. In Phil 1:1, Paul says: "Paul and Timothy, slaves of Christ Jesus." The term "slaves of Christ" means that they are devoted to the work of Christ. With this description of his work, Paul exhorts the Philippians to devote themselves to the same cause of the love of Christ. In 1 Corinthians 1:1, Paul begins with "Paul, called to be an apostle of Christ Jesus by the will of God." Given a wide array of issues at Corinth, facing various types of troublemakers in the church, Paul emphasizes his work as an apostle of Christ Jesus and by the will of God. In Rom 1:1, he begins with "Paul, a slave of Jesus Christ, called to be an apostle, set apart for the gospel of God." This beginning is most elaborate, hinting at what he is going to say to the Roman Christians. His mission is about the good news of God for which he was set apart.[1] He is an apostle who follows Jesus.

In Gal 1:1, Paul has a still different beginning: "Paul an apostle, who is not sent from human authority or commissioned through human agency, but sent through Jesus Christ and God the Father, who raised him from the dead." He vehemently defends his apostolic credentials and the truth of the gospel that he proclaimed to the Galatians. This defense implies that there

---

1. This language of "setting apart for something" belongs to prophetic callings in the Hebrew Bible (Isa 49:1; Jer 1:5). In Gal 1:15–16, Paul also says similar things that echo prophetic calling: "But when God, who had set me apart before I was born and called me through his grace, was pleased to reveal his Son to me, so that I might proclaim him among the gentiles, I did not confer with any human being."

is a challenge to his gospel. He says he is not sent by human commission (literally, "from people") or by human authorities (literally, "by people"). Indeed, he was not sent by the Jerusalem church or Jerusalem apostles. Nevertheless, he argues he is also an apostle, "sent through Jesus Christ and God the Father." His apostolic credentials are based on Jesus and God. It is not solely about Jesus or about God but about both Jesus and God. Jesus is the one who fulfilled God's promise through faith (Gal 3:22). He is the Son of God who was faithful to God and revealed God's love and justice at the risk of his life. All Jesus could do and has to do was to live according to the will of God, as implied in Gal 1:4: "[Jesus] who gave himself . . . according to the will of our God and Father." Ultimately, God is the one to whom be the glory forever (Gal 1:5). In Paul's theology, God sent his Son to the world and raised him from the dead. In other words, the ultimate source of the good news is God who sent Jesus his Son.[2] In sum, Paul's apostolic credentials are based on both God and Jesus. Paul's theology affirms the priority of God's grace before anything else. Jesus did his job faithfully according to the will of God. He gave his life to set his people free from the present evil age. Because of this, when they participate in his faithfulness, they may live a new life of freedom in the Spirit. Paul also believes that God loves all people and feels that his job as an apostle to the gentiles is to proclaim the gospel of God through Christ.

> **Consider and discuss:** As we saw above, each of Paul's letter beginnings is different. Especially, Gal 1:1 is unique in its formulation and tone. No other letter begins this way. What does this peculiar beginning have to do with the letter content? How does he achieve the goal of the letter, if any?

Paul mentions those with him, whom he includes along with himself as sending the letter, and recipients of the letter: the churches of Galatia.

---

2. For example, in 1 Cor 15:28, we see that idea of Paul: "When all things are subjected to him, then the Son himself will also be subjected to the one who put all things in subjection under him, so that God may be all in all." Here, Paul indicates that Jesus is a human messiah that yields to God on the last day. Jesus's humanity is never denied, even when he is exalted and seated in the right hand of God. Similarly, in Rom 1:4, he says Jesus was "declared to be Son of God with power according to the spirit of holiness by resurrection from the dead." The language of "to declare" suggests that Jesus became Son of God. In other words, Jesus was born as a human under the law just like any other Jew (cf. Gal 4:4). Because of his work of God, he "was crucified by weakness, but lives by the power of God" (2 Cor 13:4).

Even though he writes the letter in his name, it is sent from a group of Christians to which he belongs. His letter is not a private communication for a private audience. He writes to a group of Christians scattered throughout southern Galatia, that is within the Roman province of Galatia. "The churches of Galatia" implies that there are multiple, diverse congregations whose members are mainly uncircumcised gentile Christians. Though the location of these communities is debatable, the theory that places the churches in South Galatia (within a Roman province of Galatia) is more persuasive than that placing them in an area further north, populated with ethnic Gauls. The main supporting reason is twofold: (1) Major Roman cities in the province of Galatia such as Iconium, Lystra, and Derbe were the ones Paul visited on his first missionary journey (Acts 13–14);[3] (2) this region has a large Jewish population with their synagogues and is close to Judea (cf. Acts 13:14; 14:1). These two factors may have contributed to high tensions between Jewish culture/religion and Christian culture in this region where Jewish influence is strong and the Christian church is weak. It is possible that some Christian Jews were sent by the Jerusalem church to exert influence on gentile Christians in terms of circumcision or other Jewish practices.

In Gal 1:3, Paul says: "Grace to you and peace from God our Father and the Lord Jesus Christ." In his greetings, Paul talks about grace from God and Jesus as well. He confesses he was called through God's grace: "But when God, who had set me apart before I was born and called me through his grace, was pleased . . ." (Gal 1:15). His call is not by human commission or from human authorities (Gal 1:1). He also says justification comes through God's grace, not through the law (Gal 2:21). But grace also comes from Jesus (Gal 1:6; 5:4; 6:18). Jesus's grace has to do with his faithful life and his giving of his life for the freedom of others (Gal 1:4). The Galatians were called by God and stayed in the grace of Jesus. But some of them were confused about the gospel of Christ and forgot his grace, which is implied in Gal 5:4: "You who want to be justified by the law have cut yourselves off from Christ; you have fallen away from grace." As we see above, grace involves both God and Jesus Christ. So "Grace to you" in 1:3a indicates that the Galatians have to depend on the grace of God and Jesus as well. Then, peace comes "from God our Father and the Lord Jesus Christ" (1:3b). Peace is the result of God's grace and their dependence on it.

3. Keener, *Galatians*, 11–12.

Then, in Gal 1:4, Paul states the content of "the gospel of Christ": Jesus "who gave himself for our sins to set us free from the present evil age, according to the will of our God and Father." In this verse, we have to tackle the meaning of Christ's giving of himself for our sins. First, it does not necessarily point to traditional atonement theories: penal-substitution theory; ransom theory; satisfaction theory; propitiation or expiation theory. In Deutero-Pauline and Pastoral letters, there is a hint that Jesus's death is necessary for purifying people from their sins. For example, Titus 2:14 says: "[Jesus] it is who gave himself for us that he might redeem us from all iniquity and purify for himself a people of his own who are zealous for good deeds." Here, the author understands Jesus's death as a sin-offering. Similarly, 1 Tim 2:6 echoes this view of Jesus's death: "[Jesus] who gave himself a ransom for all—this was attested at the right time." But when it comes to Heb 10:11–14, the above idea of atonement is clearer in that Jesus's death replaces the old covenant and sacrificial system. Here, Jesus's death is also considered a sin-offering once and for all. Similarly, in 1 Pet 2:24, a similar sense of atonement is clearly evident: "He himself bore our sins in his body on the cross, so that, free from sins, we might live for righteousness; by his wounds you have been healed."

But in Paul's undisputed letters there are no decisive texts that support such views of the traditional atonement theories. Rather, Paul's usual expressions about Jesus's death in his undisputed letters and its relation to sinners are as follows: "Jesus died for our sins" (1 Cor 15:3); "he died for us" (Rom 5:8; 1 Thess 5:10; cf. Rom 8:34; 2 Cor 5:14); "he gave himself" (Gal 1:4; 2:20).[4] Unlike Hebrews, nowhere does Paul say that Jesus's one-time death resolved sin's problem once and for all, or that justification/salvation was done because of his sin sacrifice. Rather, he says that because Jesus died for all, all have died (2 Cor 5:14). In other words, Jesus's one-time death does not resolve human problems unless people die with him. For example, Paul says in Rom 8:13: "for if you live according to the flesh, you will die; but if by the Spirit you put to death the deeds of the body, you will live." As Jesus overcame sin by the Spirit, living to God, dying to sin, his followers also have to do the same.

Second, Jesus's giving of his life "for our sins" has more to do with his moral sacrifice, which is the result of his loving of God and people (Gal

---

4. Other related texts about Jesus's death are 1 Cor 1:18–25; Rom 3:21–26; 8:3–4; 2 Cor 5:21.

2:20).[5] Jesus as the Son of God was faithful to God and revealed God's righteousness in the world. He showed an example of how to deal with sin and how to live for God and the world. Because of this work, he was crucified. But because of his faithful work and his love of them, people realize they are sinners and repent and return to God. As a result, they may live a new life in Christ because they died to sin and submit to God. In Gal 2:20, Paul mentions Christ's love and his giving himself for him: "and it is no longer I who live, but it is Christ who lives in me. And the life I now live in the flesh I live by the faith of the Son of God, who loved me and gave himself for me." Because of his moral death and his love, people receive the grace of God and realize they are wrong. But that is not enough. They have to participate in his life, which means to die to sin and live to God (Rom 6:10). It also means that by the Spirit they have to put to death the deeds of the body (Rom 8:13).

If we understand Jesus's death and its relation to sin this way, it is not *"instead of* us" (substitutionary death) but *"because of* us" or *"for the sake of* us." "Because of us" implies "we sought our will and disobeyed God." The sense is that our evil or sin made him die. "For the sake of us" implies that his death is for our benefit. While we were selfish, he showed a great example of love, which is to give his life for the freedom of people from the evil age. In this sense, "for our sins," which appears only here and 1 Cor 15:3 within Paul's letters, may be interchangeable with "for us," as in Rom 5:8 and 1 Thess 5:10. Jesus's exemplary life and his love will be a driving force for people to live a new life in Christ and move away from sin. The human problem is they are defeated by sin because of their sinful passions. The solution is to die to sin. Then they may live to God and follow the way of Christ. Otherwise, Jesus's death does not remove their sins.

Third, Jesus's giving of himself for our sins has a purpose: "to set us free from the present evil age." Jesus's death alone is not sufficient to overcome sin because people have to die with him. Dying with him means to die to sin, which then means "by the Spirit to put to death the deeds of the body" (Rom 8:13). When they do so, they may be set free from the law of sin. Here, freedom does not mean one can do anything or point to a status of free will. Rather, this freedom is a total binding to God or full submission to God. In other words, freedom is possible when one does not become a slave of sin. Romans 6–7 is helpful to understand the relationship between

5. The following texts can be also interpreted from the perspective of moral sacrifice: 1 Cor 15:3; 2 Cor 5:21; Rom 5:6–10; 8:3–4.

freedom and sin.[6] Christ died to sin (Rom 6:10). His death to sin means sin as power does not rule or dominate him.[7] This also means he was not defeated by sin. Rather, he fought it by the Spirit and resisted its evil power. He chose to live to God and died to sin. Because Christ showed this great example of his life and death, his followers have to do the same thing. Romans 6:4–6 confirms this point:

> 4 Therefore we have been buried with him by baptism into death, so that, just as Christ was raised from the dead by the glory of the Father, so we too might walk in newness of life. 5 For if we have been united with him in a death like his, we will certainly be united with him in a resurrection like his. 6 We know that our old self was crucified with him so that the body of sin might be destroyed, and we might no longer be enslaved to sin.

In Rom 6:6, our old self means sin-ruled life or body, and freedom is to get out of sin. The only way to avoid sin is to follow the way of Christ. Since sin is power and rules the body, it is not removed from the world. It can be dealt with by the way of Christ. That is, he did not submit to sin or evil. An analogy may be helpful; it is like pulling sin's plug from the socket to the body. Paul explains this in Rom 6:11–13:

> 11 So you also must consider yourselves dead to sin and alive to God in Christ Jesus. 12 Therefore, do not let sin exercise dominion in your mortal bodies, to make you obey their passions. 13 No longer present your members to sin as instruments of wickedness, but present yourselves to God as those who have been brought from death to life, and present your members to God as instruments of righteousness.

Understood this way, "the present evil age," which appears only here in the New Testament, may be better understood as the status of the time and

---

6. See Kim, *Preaching the New Testament Again*.

7. "Sin" appears most frequently in Romans: Rom 3:9, 20; 4:8; 5:12f., 16, 20; 6:1f., 6, 10, 20, 22; 7:7ff., 11, 13, 17, 20, 23, 25; 8:2f., 10; 14:23. It also appears in his other letters: 1 Cor 6:18; 7:28, 36; 8:12; 15:34, 56; 2 Cor 5:21; 11:7; Gal 2:17; 3:22. It also appears in other non-Pauline letters: 1 Tim 5:20; Heb 3:13; 4:15; 9:26, 28; 10:2f., 6, 8, 18, 26; 11:25; 12:1, 4; 13:11; 1 Pet 2:22; 4:1; 2 Pet 2:14. "Sins" is different from "sin" in the sense that the latter is power while the former is the result of sinning. "Sins" also appears frequently in Pauline and other non-Pauline letters: Rom 3:25; 4:7; 5:14; 11:27; 1 Cor 6:18; 15:3, 17; Gal 1:4; Col 1:14; 1 Thess 2:16; 1 Tim 5:22, 24; 2 Tim 3:6; Heb 1:3; 2:17; 5:1, 3; 7:27; 8:12; 9:7, 22, 28; 10:4, 11, 17, 26; 1 Pet 2:24; 3:18; 4:8; 2 Pet 1:9.

place that sin rules.[8] Sin is prevalent, and people are evil without seeking God's will. Sin rules the world, people, hearts, and minds. It permeates everywhere and pervades all spheres of human life. The "evil age" is then none other than the time that sin rules. "Present" is added to emphasize the effect of sin's power in the present. Sin is everywhere, and people are so vulnerable that they become slaves of sin. The only way to get out of this dilemma is to die to sin and die with Christ.

Finally, Jesus's giving of himself for our sins to set us free from the present evil age is done "according to the will of our God and Father," the formula of which is a bit different from other letters of Paul, in which "the will of God" alone appears.[9] But here "the will of our God and Father" is a unique form, and Paul seems to emphasize the importance of Christ's work this way. He also claims that it is by "the will of our God and Father" that Jesus lived and died his life. His life is "for our sins" (that is, "because of our sins") to set us free from the sin-ruled age. Jesus's death is because people did not seek God's will. When his followers participate in his death and life, they may be free from the sin-ruled age.[10] As Jesus was obedient to God's will, they also must live for it. Then, they can be free from the evil age.[11] In other words, they have to live by faith and put to death the deeds of the body (Rom 8:13). Then they may not be defeated by sin and live to God.

Sin and Freedom

For Paul, sin is a power and is pervasive. It cannot be removed from the world until the parousia. Jesus died to sin and lived to God. Dying to sin means he was not defeated by sin. Sin tempted

---

8. "The present evil age" is often understood apocalyptically in that Jesus defeated evil once and for all through his death. It is also understood through ransom theory in that Jesus's death is a ransom to deliver people from the hands of the devil. But an alternative view of Jesus's moral sacrifice makes better sense, as we see in this book.

9. See for example: Rom 8:20, 27; 12:2; 1 Cor 1:1; 2 Cor 1:1; 8:5; 1 Thess 4:3; 5:18. Also see other letters: Eph 1:1; 5:17; 6:6; Col 1:1; 2 Tim 1:1.

10. See Cosgrove, *The Cross and the Spirit*, 172–94. He emphasizes participation in Christ's death and his lordship.

11. Paul's language of "free from something" appears also in Rom 6:7–8, 17–18, 22 ("free from sin"), in Rom 7:3–6 ("free from the law"), and in Rom 7:23, 25; 8:1–2 ("free from the law of sin"). In all of these, he does not suggest that Christ's death is enough for believers so that they may be free from the law, sin, or death, as understood in traditional atonement theories. Rather, his point is that freedom is possible for them when they participate in Christ's faith; this is because Christ defeated sin by dying to it. For more about this, see Yung Suk Kim, *Rereading Romans from the Perspective of Paul's Gospel.*

> or tested him, but it could not defeat him because he sought to do
> God's will. He revealed God's love and justice at the risk of his life.
> All those who follow Jesus will be set right with God. Galatians 1:4
> conveys the above idea: Jesus "who gave himself for our sins to set
> us free from the present evil age, according to the will of our God
> and Father."

1:6–10 CONFUSION ABOUT THE GOSPEL

6 I am astonished that you are so quickly deserting the one who
called you in the grace of Christ and are turning to a different gospel— 7 not that there is another gospel, but there are some who are
confusing you and want to change the gospel of Christ. 8 But even
if we or an angel from heaven should proclaim to you a gospel contrary to what we proclaimed to you, let that one be under a curse!
9 As we have said before, so now I repeat, if anyone proclaims to
you a gospel contrary to what you received, let that one be under a
curse! 10 Am I trying to win over human beings or God? Or am I
trying to please people? If I were still pleasing people, I would not
be a slave of Christ.

Now, in Gal 1:6–10, Paul abruptly shifts to the main topic of the letter without giving any thanksgiving to the Galatians. In fact, in Gal 1:1–5, he implied the topic of the letter when he talked about the significance of Christ's
work and his independent apostleship. But here in Gal 1:6, he is explicit
about the occasion of the letter and the topic, which is about the gospel: "I
am astonished that you are so quickly deserting the one who called you in
the grace of Christ and is turning to a different gospel."[12] He is astonished
because some Galatians deserted the one who called them in the grace of
Christ. He relates God's work to Christ's. God is the one who called them
in Christ's grace. Otherwise, he does not say God called them through his
grace alone. God is graceful, but he needs Christ (Messiah) and his work of
grace. Christ's grace is a gift of his life and service for the world. Typically,
scholars see the grace of God alone in Paul's letters and rarely talk about
Christ's grace at all. But here in Gal 1:6, we have a genitive case: "*en chariti*

---

12. "You" in this verse seems to point to all Galatians. But obviously, not all Galatians
moved away from Paul's teaching. In fact, in 1:7, he refers to "some who are confusing
you and want to pervert the gospel of Christ."

Christou." Though there are textual variants and *Christou* is missing in some traditions, given the trusting witnesses of manuscript traditions, "*en chariti Christou*" is to be preferred.[13] Now the issue is how to translate or interpret this genitive phrase: (1) a subjective genitive ("Christ's grace") or, (2) an objective genitive ("a grace from or in Christ"). In the history of interpretation, typically, what has been emphasized about Christ is not his grace but his life as a gift from God. From Augustine to Luther and up to now, the mainline theology of Paul is to emphasize the grace of God in Christ and the Christ-event itself. Otherwise, there is no substantial articulation on Christ's grace and his faithfulness. In this regard, John Barclay's recent book *Paul and the Gift* is not different and does not see the importance of Christ's grace.[14] Against some traditional views of grace that emphasize only "incongruity, singularity, or noncircularity," he adds God's judgment to God's grace and emphasizes believers' participation in the Christ-event.[15] In his terms, "incongruity" means humans are unworthy of receiving the grace of God. "Singularity" means that God is absolutely loving and not judgmental, and "noncircularity" means that basically, the gift (grace) is free and there is no requirement for human action. Barclay's view of grace strikes a balance between God's grace and human participation, but he does not consider the agency of Christ and his faithfulness. Likewise, he does not see Christ's grace in Gal 1:6 and elsewhere. Christ's faithfulness and human agency as the Messiah must be an important element in Paul's gospel. Indeed, Paul's benediction usually ends with "The grace of our Lord Jesus Christ be with you" (Gal 6:18; Rom 16:20; 2 Cor 13:13; Phil 4:23; 1 Thess 5:28; Phlm 1:25), and this grace must be Christ's.

Jesus did his job of demonstrating God's righteousness through faith (cf. Rom 3:22). God was pleased with him because of his Son's faithfulness. The Galatians received this grace of Jesus and they were called by God. Therefore, they have to participate in his faith so that they may have a good relationship with God (cf. Gal 2:16–21; 3:21–22; Rom 3:22). That is what justification means in Paul's theology.

"A different gospel" (*heteros euangelion*) implies that this gospel may not be wrong but simply different. It may be understood as a different form of the gospel in a Jewish setting that Jews can keep laws such as the circumcision while staying in the faith of Christ. But this different gospel cannot

13. See Metzger, *A Textual Commentary on the Greek New Testament*, 589–90.

14. Barclay, *Paul and the Gift*, 351–446.

15. Barclay, *Paul and the Gift*, 66–78.

be imposed onto the gentile Christians. If circumcision is forced on the Galatians, this gospel is not a different one but a wrong one. All proclamations that are not based on Christ crucified are not the truth of the gospel.[16] In the context of Galatia, this different gospel may be wrong because Christian Jews claim that law observance or works of the law are to be kept without conditions. This gospel is different from Paul's gospel and wrong because justification is made only through the faith of Christ Jesus (Gal 2:16).[17] This does not mean the law is wrong or the works of the law are useless; the issue is whether faith is a *prime* thing that interprets and fulfills the law. It is true that Paul uses the law or "works of the law" negatively in Galatians in some sense.[18] But this negative use in Galatians must be understood within the Galatian context where Paul contrasts faith with the absolutism of the law, especially pertaining to circumcision. Otherwise, he does not reject the law itself or the works of the law because of faith (cf. Rom 3:31). For Paul, the issue is how to interpret the law, and he interprets it through the lens of love, as he summarizes in Gal 5:14: "For the whole law is summed up in a single commandment, 'You shall love your neighbor as yourself.'" In sum, the problem occurs when the law is interpreted apart from faith or when the works of the law take over faith.

Therefore, if the law and faith are understood together in ways that the law is interpreted through faith and that it is fulfilled through love, the law and faith can go hand in hand. Furthermore, he says that faith cannot overthrow the law: "Do we then overthrow the law by this faith? By no means! On the contrary, we uphold the law" (Rom 3:31; cf. Rom 7:12). So he says the law must be upheld, and he thinks the essence of the law is the love of neighbor (Gal 5:14; Rom 13:8–10).

> **Consider and discuss:** Given the fact that Paul uses "a different gospel" rather than a wrong gospel, do you think he allows for a different version of the gospel for Jews? If so, what is the form of the gospel he imagines for them? Does he allow for two different gospels, one for the Jews and one for the gentiles? If the essence of

---

16. Paul's gospel emphasizes Christ crucified; for example, see Gal 2:19; 5:24; 6:14; 1 Cor 1:23; 2:2.

17. Richard Hays is one of the early proponents of the subjective genitive reading of *pistis christou*. See Hays, *The Faith of Jesus Christ*.

18. For example, see Gal 2:16, 19, 21; 3:2, 5, 10, 17, 21, 23; 4:4f., 21; 5:3f., 14, 18, 23; 6:2, 13.

> the gospel is one and the same for Jews and gentiles, how can you describe this nature of the common gospel for both?

But there is some confusion about the gospel in the Galatian situation because some people argue that gentile Christians must be circumcised. Circumcision is part of the law and "the works of the law," and it is important to Jews because it is a covenantal sign for them (Gen 17:1–14). It is mandatory for all Jewish males. So some Christian Jews insist that this part of the law must apply to the gentiles. In other words, they say faith alone is not enough. But Paul's interpretation of the law is different. He argues that Abraham's faith (Gen 12) comes *before* his circumcision (Gen 17). What makes one justified is not the law but one's faith that upholds the law. Paul's argument is that circumcision is good for Jews and that they may keep this tradition along with the faith of Jesus. In this limited sense, Paul may have called this Jewish gospel "a different gospel." But that law of circumcision should not be imposed on gentile Christians because his worry is that they may be pushed to keep all laws, including Jewish culture. His concern is well stated in Gal 5:3: "Once again I testify to every man who lets himself be circumcised that he is obliged to obey the entire law." He goes on to say in Gal 5:4: "You who want to be justified by the law have cut yourselves off from Christ; you have fallen away from grace."

Then in Gal 1:7, Paul clarifies his phrase "a different gospel": "not that there is another gospel, but there are some who are confusing you and want to pervert the gospel of Christ." He says there are some who are confusing other members, and these people have a zeal for the law and circumcision and prioritize the law or the works of the law over faith.[19] Confusion is about whether Christians need faith only or faith and the law together. Paul's argument is, as noted before, faith comes before the law, and then the former must inform the latter. Moreover, this faith models after Jesus who was faithful to God. Paul's Christian Jewish "opponents" do not see the importance of faith and its relation to the law. That is the same as perverting "the gospel of Christ." They do not see the work of Christ that constitutes the gospel of Christ, as implied in Gal 1:4: "Jesus gave himself for our sins to set us free from the present evil age, according to the will of our God and

---

19. John Barclay talks about the benefit of circumcision for gentile Christians who want to secure their social identity by converting to Judaism. That is, recent converts felt precarious about their identity and so readily accepted circumcision, which is the Jewish custom. See Barclay, *Obeying the Truth*, 58–60.

Father." Jesus obeyed God's will that his people be set free from the present evil age, and he gave himself for them because of his love. Jesus's obedience of God's will has to do with his proclamation of God's good news in the sense that God is good news, love, hope, and resurrection. In this sense, "the gospel of Christ" is the gospel that he proclaimed, which is "the good news about God."[20] But at the same time, "the gospel of Christ" means the good news about Christ because he did good things for the world. In other words, when people hear of his obedient faith toward God and his love for them, they may change their mind toward God. They may follow him and live a new life in the Spirit. This is the good news about him. Otherwise, the gospel of Christ is not salvific knowledge about him.

Paul knows Jesus was faithful to God until he died. Therefore, he wants to live by Christ's faith, not merely by faith in Christ. He states this resolutely later in Gal 2:20: "and it is no longer I who live, but it is Christ who lives in me. And the life I now live in the flesh I live by *the faith of the Son of God, who loved me and gave himself for me*." He confesses that Christ lived faithfully as the Son of God ("faith of the Son of God," which must be a subjective genitive) and thus he also wants to follow him, living by his (Christ's) faith.[21] He also confesses that Christ loved him and gave himself for him. This is the good news about Christ.

"The Gospel of Christ"

"The gospel of Christ" is a very important theme throughout Paul's undisputed letters. With this phrase, Paul elevates Christ's faith and his grace (1 Cor 9:12; 2 Cor 9:13; Phil 1:27; and 1 Thess 3:2). In 1 Cor 9:12, he points to "the way of the gospel of Christ" in

---

20. "Good news of God" appears in Rom 1:1; 15:16 and 1 Thess 2:2, 8. But it is also implied in Galatians because Jesus obeyed God's will (1:4–5). His work of God is about the good news of God that involves liberation, new life, justice, and peace. For this good news of God, Jesus gave his life to liberate people from the evil age according to the will of God.

21. *Pistis christou* appears in Gal 2:16, 20; 3:22; Rom 3:22, 25–26; Phil 3:9. All these occurrences can be understood as using a subjective genitive. Paul always looks to Christ's faith first and then Christians' participation in him. For example, in Gal 2:16, he talks about Christ's faith through which one is justified, and because of his faith as such, his followers need to *believe into Christ* (*pisteuo eis christon*). As "the faith of Abraham" in Rom 4:16 is construed as Abraham's faith, *pistis christou* must be also the faith of Christ. Christ's faith means his obedience to God's will that God's righteousness may be revealed and that his people may be set free from the evil age. See also Phil 2:6–11 and Rom 5:12–21 where Jesus's obedient faith is seen. Martyn sees Christ's faith in Gal 2:16–20 as his faithful death. See Martyn, "A Law-observant Messiah to the Gentiles," 307–24.

his response to those who belittle his ministry in the Corinthian church. Other missionaries elevated their own achievements along with their privileges. But Paul talks about the example of Christ and his way of life in proclaiming the gospel of God. Similarly, in 2 Cor 9:13, Paul exhorts the Corinthians to be obedient to "the gospel of Christ" by sharing the generosity with others. Philippians 1:27 is more straightforward in its emphasis on Christ's work and his manner of life: "Only, live your life in a manner worthy of the gospel of Christ, so that, whether I come and see you or am absent and hear about you, I will know that you are standing firm in one spirit, striving side by side with one mind for the faith of the gospel." In Philippians, Paul talks about Christ's sacrifice, his love, and faith. What Christ did and what he lived for constitute "the gospel of Christ." He is an example of faith and foundation of the church, as 1 Cor 3:11 says: "For no one can lay any foundation other than the one that has been laid; that foundation is Jesus Christ." In 1 Thess 3:2, Paul talks about Timothy's work that has to do with "proclaiming the gospel of Christ," which is also understood in line with Christ's work and his grace. Lastly, in Romans, the gospel of Christ is similar to the form "the gospel concerning his Son" (Rom 1:3), which is what he did: the demonstration of God's righteousness through faith (Rom 3:22).

In Gal 1:8–9, Paul condemns and curses those who proclaim a gospel contrary to what he has proclaimed. No one, including himself and even an angel, can proclaim a gospel that elevates the law or "the works of the law" at the expense of faith. Paul's point here is not that he has more power than the Galatians. His curse language of "let that one be under a curse!" expresses his concern about their situation where a wrong gospel obviates the work of Christ and of the Spirit. The gospel depends on the grace of God and Jesus's work of grace according to the will of God. Otherwise, even an angel from heaven can add more to the gospel. Paul's point is the gospel is bigger than he or anyone else. What is proclaimed to the Galatians is not from him but the gospel. In fact, they received the gospel gladly and experienced its power before they were urged to undergo circumcision.

In Gal 1:10, Paul concludes the letter's opening and says: "Am I now seeking human approval, or God's approval? Or am I trying to please people? If I were still pleasing people, I would not be a servant of Christ." This verse refers back to Gal 1:1 where he says he is "not sent from human authority or commissioned through human agency, but sent through Jesus

Christ and God the Father, who raised him from the dead." The problem occurs when there is only human approval without God's approval. When there is a conflict between God's approval and human approval, one must choose the former. Otherwise, Paul's point is not that he does not need approval or understanding about his gospel from people. That is why he attends the Jerusalem Council to clear up unnecessary misunderstandings about his gospel.

SECTION II

1:11–24

The Origin of the Gospel

AFTER THE LETTER'S OPENING (Gal 1:1–10), Paul talks about the origin of his gospel in Gal 1:11–24. He insists his gospel is not of human origin but based on God's revelation of Jesus Christ (Gal 1:11–17). God is the source of his gospel, and its content is about Christ. Then, he states his gospel does not depend on the Jerusalem apostles (Gal 1:18–24). He makes clear that his gospel is from God and that it is not of human origin, the result of education, or the teaching of a particular tradition or place. His point is not that his gospel is based on his special experience with God or with Jesus but that God revealed his Son to him. When Paul talks about a revelation about Jesus from God, the Galatians may have thought that he was bragging about his special experience. But if we read the letter as a whole, what he tries to show is not done to establish his reputation or special experience as such, but to tell his readers that *the origin of his gospel is God*. He is confident about this gospel and needs to defend it to the churches of Galatia.

1:11–17 GOD'S REVELATION OF JESUS CHRIST

11 Brothers and sisters, I want you to know that the gospel that I proclaimed is not of human origin; 12 for I did not receive it from a human source, nor was I taught it, but I received it through a revelation of Jesus Christ. 13 You have heard, no doubt, of my earlier life in Judaism. I was violently persecuting the church of God and was trying to destroy it. 14 I advanced in Judaism beyond

29

many among my people of the same age, for I was far more zealous for the traditions of my ancestors. 15 But when God, who had set me apart before I was born and called me through his grace, was pleased 16 to reveal his Son to me, so that I might proclaim him among the gentiles, I did not confer with any human being, 17 nor did I go up to Jerusalem to those who were already apostles before me, but I went away at once into Arabia, and afterwards I returned to Damascus.

Paul says his gospel ("the gospel he proclaimed") is not "according to humans" (*kata anthrōpon*, Gal 1:11). In other words, the source of his gospel is God, not humans. Moreover, he says he did not receive the gospel from humans (*para anthrōpou*), which would mean a human origin for the gospel. He also says he was not taught it, which also signifies his main source of the gospel is God. He explains the source of the gospel three times with negative expressions: "not according to humans," "not from humans," and "not taught it." All the above negative expressions do not mean that he did not have any contact with other Christians or learn anything from them (cf. 1 Cor 15:1–3). His point is the origin of the gospel is not human agency but God. The gospel comes *from God* and it is about him.

In Gal 1:12, Paul says he received the gospel "through a revelation of Jesus Christ." We tend to think that Jesus Christ appeared to Paul and told him all about the truth or a special revelation about God or the world. This image of Paul is found in Acts 9:1–19, which is not Paul's own account. In his own account of Gal 1:15–16, he says God revealed his Son to (or in) him. The Book of Acts dramatizes Paul's conversion experience and highlights his encounter with Christ. But in his own account, he just mentions God's revelation of his Son. In fact, "a revelation of Jesus Christ" (1:12) can be taken as an objective genitive, "a revelation *about* Jesus," because God revealed his Son to him. The origin of the gospel is God and it comes through God's revelation of Jesus.

> **Consider and discuss:** We usually think Paul met the risen Lord on the way to Damascus and received a revelation from him. This understanding comes from Acts' account. But in Gal 1:15–16, he says God revealed his Son in (or to) him. God is the revealer of Jesus, but we do not know how it happened or what Jesus did at this time of revelation. In Gal 1:12, he says he received the gospel through "a revelation of Jesus," which is ambiguous since it is the genitive case and involves two possibilities: "Jesus's revelation" or

"a revelation about Jesus." What do you think Paul means? If he means the former, then Paul's Damascus road experience in Acts makes sense. But if he means the latter, the revealer is not Jesus but God. What do you think?

Then, in Gal 1:13–14, he says: "You have heard, no doubt, of my earlier life in Judaism. I was violently persecuting the church of God and was trying to destroy it. I advanced in Judaism beyond many among my people of the same age, for I was far more zealous for the traditions of my ancestors." He was so confident about his belief that Jesus cannot be the Jewish Messiah. He thought that the followers of Jesus were wrong because they did not follow conventional interpretations of Jewish tradition and law. So he "was violently persecuting the church of God and was trying to destroy it" (1:13).[1]

Consider and discuss: In Gal 1:13, Paul says he persecuted "the church of God." In his undisputed letters, he uses "the church of God" whenever he refers to the church. Why does he not say "the church of Christ"? Paul perhaps thinks that while the church belongs to God, Christ is the foundation of it. Then, in what sense does he think Christ is the foundation of the church in Galatia?

In Gal 1:15–16, Paul talks about a life-changing event for him. When God called him and revealed his Son to him, he could change his mind about Jesus and God. His calling is to let the world know that Jesus is the Son of God through whom people may turn to God and live a new life in the Spirit. When God called him, he was given the task of proclaiming the good news of God and the good news of Christ among the gentiles (Gal 1:16). Otherwise, he does not proclaim merely what he heard from other Christians. His consistent thinking is that *God is the source of the gospel* (Gal 1:15). God revealed his Son to or in Paul.

In sum, what Paul tries to say to the Galatians is this: The gospel he proclaimed to them is not based on Jewish tradition or his special experience with God. God revealed his Son to Paul and the content of revelation is about Jesus, "who gave himself for our sins to set us free from the present

1. Interestingly here, he calls the gathering of Christians "the church of God," not the church of Christ. For Paul, the church is God's and Christ is the foundation of the church. For example, see the following examples: 1 Cor 1:2; 10:32; 11:22; 15:9; 2 Cor 1:1; Gal 1:13.

evil age, according to the will of our God and Father," as indicated in Gal 1:4. Because of this revelation, he changed his view of God, Christ, and the children of God. Previously, he thought that God is the God of Jews only, that the Messiah must be someone like David, and that children of God must be Abraham's biological descendants who keep the law.[2] But now he understands God is the God of both Jews *and gentiles*; Jesus Christ is the long-awaited Messiah who gave himself to set *all* people free from the present evil age.

Because of this new revelation of the gospel, Paul could not stay home but went away at once into Arabia, which is believed to be the Nabatean lands close to Damascus. (For the Arabia of Mount Sinai is too far from Damascus.) We do not know what he did there. But most probably, he shared the good news of God and the good news of Jesus Christ with local people there. After that, he came back to Damascus and continued to share his gospel with others. For this gospel, he says in Gal 1:16b–17, "I did not confer with any human being, nor did I go up to Jerusalem to those who were already apostles before me." Again, his point is simply that his gospel is not based on any human being or human source and that he did not go up to Jerusalem to be anointed or authorized by the apostles there.

1:18–24 INDEPENDENT OF JERUSALEM CHURCHES

> 18 Then after three years I went up to Jerusalem to visit Cephas and stayed with him fifteen days; 19 but I did not see any other apostle except James the Lord's brother. 20 Before God, I'm not lying about the things that I'm writing to you! 21 Then I went into the regions of Syria and Cilicia, 22 and I was still unknown by sight to the churches of Judea that are in Christ; 23 they only heard it said, "The one who formerly was persecuting us is now proclaiming the faith he once tried to destroy." 24 And they glorified God because of me.

In 1:18, Paul states that after three years, he went up to Jerusalem to visit Cephas and stayed with him fifteen days. "After three years" must be three

---

2. In Rom 3:30, Paul affirms that God is the God of *all*: "Or is God the God of Jews only? Is he not the God of gentiles also? Yes, of gentiles also." In Jewish tradition, someone crucified on a cross cannot be a messiah (cf. Deut 21:22–23); rather, such a death would be a case of failure as a messiah. Children of God are descendants of Abraham who stay in the covenantal community by keeping the law.

years after his reception of a revelation about Christ (cf. Gal 1:12). According to Acts 9, he went up to Jerusalem immediately after his conversion. This is because Acts wants to portray him as an ideal missionary who is led by the Spirit and confirmed by Jerusalem churches. But here in Galatians, Paul says he did not go to Jerusalem immediately after he received a revelation. It took three years for even a short casual visit to Cephas. We do not know what Paul and Peter did or talked about when they stayed together. Then, in Gal 1:19, Paul emphasizes that he did not see any other apostle except James the Lord's brother and swears that he did not lie about this (Gal 1:20). All he wants to say here is he did not consult any particular apostle about his gospel. After a short visit to Cephas in Jerusalem, Paul went into the regions of Syria and Cilicia to share his gospel (Gal 1:21).

In Gal 1:22–24, Paul says that at the time of his visit he was not well known in Jerusalem and nearby. However, they knew that "the one who formerly was persecuting us is now proclaiming the faith he once tried to destroy" (Gal 1:23). Nevertheless, his gospel was received well, as the churches of Judea glorified God because of him (Gal 1:24).

SECTION III

2:1–21

The Clarification of the Gospel

IN THE PREVIOUS SECTION (Gal 1:11–24), we saw the origin of Paul's gospel, which is God's revelation of Jesus Christ. Otherwise, it is not by humans or from humans. In this section, Gal 2:1–21, Paul clarifies his gospel in relation to Jewish laws and customs. While his gospel does not depend on Jerusalem apostles, he wants them to understand it. So he attends the Council of Jerusalem so that he may focus on proclaiming the gospel to the gentiles. There was a consensus between him and the Jerusalem apostles. However, sometime later his expectation of Jerusalem apostles collapses because of an incident in Antioch where Peter avoids having table-fellowship with gentiles when certain people came from James. Because of this issue, Paul clarifies his gospel in relation to Jewish law and "the works of the law." He argues that the right relationship with God (which is the concept of "justification") is not based on "the works of the law" such as circumcision or dietary regulations but through the faithfulness of Jesus Christ.

2:1–10 THE GOSPEL AT THE COUNCIL OF JERUSALEM

1 Then after fourteen years I went up again to Jerusalem with Barnabas, taking Titus along with me. 2 I went up in response to a revelation. Then I laid before them (though only in a private meeting with the acknowledged leaders) the gospel that I proclaim among the gentiles, in order to make sure that I was not running, or had not run, in vain. 3 But even Titus, who was with me, was

not compelled to be circumcised, though he was a Greek. 4 But because of false believers secretly brought in, who slipped in to spy on the freedom we have in Christ Jesus, so that they might enslave us— 5 we did not submit to them even for a moment, so that the truth of the gospel might always remain with you. 6 And from those who were supposed to be acknowledged leaders (what they actually were makes no difference to me; God shows no partiality)—those leaders contributed nothing to me. 7 On the contrary, when they saw that I had been entrusted with the gospel for the uncircumcised, just as Peter had been entrusted with the gospel for the circumcised 8 (for he who worked through Peter making him an apostle to the circumcised also worked through me in sending me to the gentiles), 9 and when James and Cephas and John, who were acknowledged pillars, recognized the grace that had been given to me, they gave to Barnabas and me the right hand of fellowship, agreeing that we should go to the gentiles and they to the circumcised. 10 They asked only one thing, that we remember the poor, which was actually what I was eager to do.

Even though his gospel or his apostleship does not depend on Jerusalem apostles, Paul is concerned about them because the gospel is one and for all people. Therefore, he needs their understanding of his gospel and their support for his ministry. While his mission is primarily for the gentiles, he firmly believes that the gospel as the power of God must be for both Jews and gentiles (cf. Rom 1:16). He also thinks of his role as a bridge-builder between Jews and gentiles. He wants to help the poor saints in Jerusalem and asks his gentile congregations to collect offerings for them. Indeed, Paul was very intentional about this collection project and was eager to deliver gifts to them. In this way, he thinks the gentile churches can pay back for the Jewish roots of the gospel. He also thinks of his job as taking the gentile Christians to Jerusalem on the last day. This idea is implied in Rom 15:16: "[Paul] to be a minister of Christ Jesus to the gentiles in the priestly service of the gospel of God, so that the offering of the gentiles may be acceptable, sanctified by the Holy Spirit." He considers himself as a priest who serves God by way of offering the gentiles to God. He also believes that God's church must be one, seeking a union of solidarity within the community rather than a hierarchical unity in the community. While individual churches are diverse and scattered along the line of region, culture, or ethnicity, the church is one; it is God's household. So for Paul, it is important to have a good relationship with the Jews or Jerusalem churches.

Considering the above contexts in his ministry, Paul decided to attend the Council of Jerusalem, which took place fourteen years after his call from God. Otherwise, he did not immediately go up to Jerusalem to talk about his ministry. When he received the gospel about Jesus Christ and when God revealed his Son to him, rather he went to the Nabatean lands and other areas to share the gospel that he received (Gal 1:16–17). Before this apostolic meeting, he spent fourteen years doing his independent work. He has experienced the power of the gospel in his gentile mission. During this time he has also experienced hardships and difficulties within and outside of the church. Among these, one of the gravest issues may have to do with pressure placed on Paul to require his gentiles audiences to follow Jewish law.

In this apostolic meeting, Paul earnestly explained his gospel to the Jerusalem leaders to make sure that he was "not running, or had not run, in vain" (Gal 2:2). The meeting seemed successful because Titus, who was with Paul, "was not compelled to be circumcised, though he was a Greek" (Gal 2:3). But some false believers secretly came to the meeting to "spy on the freedom we have in Christ Jesus so that they might enslave us" (Gal 2:4). But he says: "We did not submit to them even for a moment, so that the truth of the gospel might always remain with you" (Gal 2:5). Paul and his companions (Barnabas and Titus) did not accept their views about the gospel. They were not shaken by them even for a moment because for them the gospel is the power of God that gives them freedom. The gospel is "the power of God for salvation to everyone who has faith, to the Jew first and also to the Greek." That power has to do with freedom and a new life in the Spirit. All people may experience freedom and new life through faith. This is "the truth of the gospel" that must remain with the Galatians (Gal 2:5). When the Galatians accept the love of God by the grace of Jesus and live by the Spirit, they are free in God and Christ. No one can chain them into the slavery of anything because freedom is granted by God. This power of the gospel is confirmed at the council, as Paul says the famous leaders from Jerusalem did not add anything to his preaching (Gal 2:6).

In Gal 2:7–10, Paul reports the good result of the Jerusalem Council. First of all, there was an agreement about the division of labor: Peter being entrusted with the gospel for the circumcised (meaning Jews) and Paul sent to the gentiles. James, Peter, and John, who were "acknowledged pillars" recognized the good work of Paul and Barnabas and agreed about the division of work between the gospel for Jews and the gospel for gentiles. (Note that there are not two different gospels: one for Jews and one for gentiles.) But the Jerusalem apostles asked only one thing: that their poor people must be remembered. Paul is eager to help them and carries out this mission throughout his gentile mission.

Consider and discuss: While Paul argues his apostleship and his gospel are not based on Jerusalem churches and apostles therein, he is still concerned about them. Why do you think it is important for him to have a good relationship with them? Does his decision to attend the apostolic council represent his weakening position on his gospel or to the Jerusalem churches?

2:11–14 THE INCIDENT AT ANTIOCH

11 But when Cephas came to Antioch, I opposed him to his face, because he stood self-condemned; 12 for until certain people came from James, he used to eat with the gentiles. But after they came, he drew back and kept himself separate for fear of the circumcision faction. 13 And the other Jews joined him in this hypocrisy, so that even Barnabas was led astray by their hypocrisy. 14 But when I saw that they were not acting consistently with the truth of the gospel, I said to Cephas in front of everyone, "If you, though you are a Jew, live like a gentile and not like a Jew, how can you compel the gentiles to live like Jews?"

Peter came to Antioch of Syria, one of the largest cities in the Roman world with increasing commerce and a huge population of about a half million.[1] A significant number of Jews lived in this city since the second century BCE, forming strong Jewish communities and developing Hellenistic Judaism. Also, this city became a center of early Christian activities (cf. Acts 11:26). Peter used to eat with the gentiles and had a fellowship with them. But when certain people came from James, the brother of Jesus in Jerusalem, he suddenly avoided eating with gentiles because he was fearful of the circumcision faction (Gal 1:12). The circumcision faction, literally "those from circumcision" emphasizes the primacy of Jewish laws and customs in the church. Beyond this, we do not know where James's people came from and who they were. They could come from Jerusalem or locally from

---

1. Keener, *Galatians: A Commentary*, 143–44.

Galatia. If they were local, they were most likely Christian Jews or some other gentile Christians who adhered to the Jewish law.

Even though Paul's mission was officially endorsed at the Jerusalem Council, the Jerusalem situation or church remained conservative toward the Jewish law and culture. That is why some came from James to spy on him. Their primary task is to watch Paul and his work and persuade gentile Christians to undergo circumcision or to practice Jewish laws. They did not come to check on Peter. But interestingly, the one who has fear is Peter himself. Paul is adamant about his gospel and he is not shaken by them at all. But Peter has fear about them, not being consistent in his own bold fellowship with the gentiles. In fact, it is not wrong for him to eat with the gentiles unless he violates dietary laws or purity laws.[2] Eating with them is not prohibited, and it is important for Jews living in the diaspora to maintain their social life with contact with others. Why then did Peter have fear about the circumcision faction? Most likely, he wants to save his reputation as a Jewish apostle who has a strong foothold in Jerusalem. In other words, he is concerned that his contact with the gentiles might give the impression to the Jerusalem churches that he has compromised to the lifestyle of the gentiles. In other words, he worries about his position in the Jerusalem church and throughout the Jewish communities.

Initially, Peter understood the importance of fellowship with gentiles and ate with them without reservation. He once met Paul briefly long ago and later in the apostolic council, where he endorsed Paul's gentile mission. But on certain occasions when certain people came from James, he became a different person who ignored the gentiles. He proves to be hypocritical and disrespectful to the gentiles. So Paul "opposed him to his face, because he stood self-condemned" (Gal 2:11).[3] He is concerned about Peter not only because of his hypocrisy but because of his impact on other Jews, as he says in Gal 1:13: "And the other Jews joined him in this hypocrisy, so that even Barnabas was led astray by their hypocrisy." So the problem is these Jews impacted by Peter were not "acting consistently with the truth of the gospel" (Gal 2:14). The truth of the gospel is the fact that *all* people—regardless of their ethnicity, class, or gender—may sit together and eat together in the name of God and in the grace of his Son. They know this fact, but they did

2. For more about the historical context of table-fellowship, see Dunn, "The Incident at Antioch (Gal 2:11–18)," 3–57. See also Keener, *Galatians: A Commentary*, 152–54.

3. Paul gives only his perspective about the Antioch incident and rebukes Peter. Otherwise, it is difficult to know Peter's perspective. Given this limitation, here we can only examine Paul's perspective.

not practice it. So they are also hypocritical. The gospel is the power of God for salvation to *everyone* who has faith. That is why Paul responded to some Jewish "false believers" in Gal 2:5: "We did not submit to them even for a moment, so that the truth of the gospel might always remain with you."

So in Gal 2:14, Paul publicly rebukes Peter: "If you, though a Jew, live like a gentile and not like a Jew, how can you compel the gentiles to live like Jews?" He uses gentile and Jew as a metaphor; in this case, a Jew means to live as a child of God, and a gentile means to live not according to God's will. In other words, one's social or ethnic identity must match his/her behavior worthy of God's commendation. But Peter did not act consistently with the truth of the gospel because he disrespected other people whom God also loves. He wavered about his position, fearing his reputation as a pillar apostle in the Jerusalem church and the Jewish diaspora communities. Peter is not a good example for the gentiles because of his cowardice toward them, so Paul asks: "how can you compel the gentiles to live like Jews?" (Gal 2:14).

In response to Peter's inconsistent behavior with the gentiles, Paul rebukes him for the lack of the truth of the gospel for all and tells the Galatians that proper Christian identity must be transformational, overcoming locality when meeting with people of other cultures, and seeking a global identity in solidarity with one another while maintaining one's cultural identity.

Regarding transformative, multicultural identity, we can gain ideas from Gal 5:6: "For in Christ Jesus neither circumcision nor uncircumcision counts for anything; the only thing that counts is faith working through love." To be transformed, one must be "in Christ," which means following the way Christ lived. "In Christ" as a modal dative is Paul's favorite phrase in his authentic letters. Using this expression, Paul emphasizes Christ's sacrifice—not sin offering or sacrifice but his *moral* sacrifice that has to do with his love of people. That is, they may be set "free from the present evil age" (Gal 1:4), not because of his sin offering, but because of his moral sacrifice through which they realize they are wrong and may change their mind and seek a new life in Christ. In such a new life in Christ, being informed by Christ's way of life, "neither circumcision nor uncircumcision counts for anything." In other words, one needs not stick to one cultural identity or to a particular cultural tradition, because while neither of them is perfect, the more important thing to pursue is the gospel for all peoples.

Essentially, Paul's point is that what makes a person perfect is not a tradition or an identity, but "faith working through love."

Based on his inconsistent fellowship behavior with the gentiles and his lack of understanding of the truth of the gospel, Peter may not have had a thorough transformation in his life. That is maybe because he has lived in Jerusalem within the boundary of the Jewish comfort zone. He did not have the same experience as Paul, who says in 1 Cor 15:8–10: "Last of all, as to one untimely born, he appeared also to me. For I am the least of the apostles, unfit to be called an apostle, because I persecuted the church of God. But by the grace of God I am what I am, and his grace toward me has not been in vain. On the contrary, I worked harder than any of them—though it was not I, but the grace of God that is with me." Obviously, Paul may have elevated his superior position as an apostle when he wrote to the Corinthians, but at least he understood that he is nothing, which is the basis of his starting point as an apostle. Likewise, he says in 2 Cor 12:9–11, "My [the Lord's] grace is sufficient for you [Paul], for power is made perfect in weakness. So, I will boast all the more gladly of my weaknesses, so that the power of Christ may dwell in me. Therefore I am content with weaknesses, insults, hardships, persecutions, and calamities for the sake of Christ; for whenever I am weak, then I am strong." While Peter may have experienced a similar transformation to Paul, it seems that it was less thorough. But Paul had many more difficulties and hardships as he lived as a diaspora Jew, often citing such times in his letters (2 Cor 1:8–9; 4:7–12; 6:9; Rom 8:31–39).

It is evident that Paul is very flexible in his missionary attitude toward others, as he says in 1 Cor 9:20–21:

> 20 To the Jews I became as a Jew, in order to win Jews. To those under the law I became as one under the law (though I myself am not under the law) so that I might win those under the law. 21 To those outside the law I became as one outside the law (though I am not free from God's law but am under Christ's law) so that I might win those outside the law.

For Paul, proper Christian identity must be adaptable to proclaiming the gospel to all peoples. But this does not mean one gives up on one's cultural identity. But dealing with others, one must be both local and global in the sense that one must go into the culture of others. In doing so, one should not judge others or their cultures, but seek to learn from them.

> **Consider and discuss:** In the Antioch incident, Paul rebukes Peter for his wavering position about table-fellowship with the gentiles. What is Paul's real concern about this incident? What is his view of desirable identity politics in his gospel? What would be Peter's response to Paul?

2:15–21 JUSTIFICATION BY CHRIST JESUS'S FAITHFULNESS

15 We ourselves are Jews by birth and not gentile sinners; 16 yet we know that a person is set right with God not by the works of the law but through the faithfulness of Jesus Christ. And we have believed into Christ Jesus, so that we might be set right with God by the faithfulness of Christ, and not by doing the works of the law, because no one will be set right with God by the works of the law. 17 But if, in our effort to be set right with God in Christ, we ourselves have been found to be sinners, is Christ then a servant of sin? Certainly not! 18 But if I build up again the very things that I once tore down, then I demonstrate that I am a transgressor. 19 For through the law I died to the law, so that I might live to God. I have been crucified with Christ; 20 and it is no longer I who live, but it is Christ who lives in me. And the life I now live in the flesh I live by the faithfulness of the Son of God, who loved me and gave himself for me. 21 I do not nullify the grace of God; for if righteousness comes through the law, then Christ died for nothing.

> **Consider and discuss:** For Paul, faith does not reject the law or vice versa, as he says: "For the whole law is summed up in a single commandment, 'You shall love your neighbor as yourself'" (Gal 5:14). Also, he says what ultimately matters is faith and love: "For in Christ Jesus neither circumcision nor uncircumcision counts for anything; the only thing that counts is faith working through love" (Gal 5:6). What is your stance about the relation between faith and the works of the law?

In Gal 2:15–21, Paul continues to clarify the gospel regarding Jewish matters, as he says in Gal 2:15: "We ourselves are Jews by birth and not gentile sinners." Jews were privileged with the holy tradition of God and blessed to live according to God's will. In this sense, they were not like others who did not have such a tradition. Gentiles are considered sinners from their perspective because they are outside the covenant, not knowing the law. But while the Jewish religious heritage is good, it is not enough for them because justification needs faith(fulness) just like Abraham's faith(fulness) or Christ Jesus's faith(fulness). Thus, Paul says in Gal 2:16, "yet we know that a person is set right with God not by the works of the law but *through the faithfulness of Jesus Christ.*[4] And we have *believed into* Christ Jesus, so that we might be set right with God *by the faithfulness of Christ,* and not by doing the works of the law, because no one will be set right with God by the works of the law" (italics for emphasis). In this verse, we have a few issues to tackle and answer: (1) how to understand the concept of righteousness or justification; (2) how to be set right with God; (3) how to interpret *pistis christou*; (4) how to interpret "the works of the law."

Regarding the first issue, justification has been usually understood as forensic salvation. So the typical translation is: "A person is justified not by . . . but through *faith in Christ Jesus.*" The so-called doctrine of "justification by faith" comes from the forensic interpretation of this verse (cf. Rom 1:17 and 3:22). Here, justification means one receives a righteousness or that one is considered righteous or innocent though one is a sinner.[5] In both these cases, God declares a verdict of righteousness because of Jesus's vicarious death for sinners. As a result, their legal status change as if they were in a court. But the Greek verb *dikaioo* connotes a range of meanings such as "to put right with," "to be set right," and "to acquit," all of which have more to do with "a right relationship" with God than a legal status change in a court. "To be justified" or "to be made righteous" is relational language in that the issue is how one may be considered "right" with God or how one can live faithfully to God. That is why Paul quotes from Hab 2:4 and says, "The righteous one will live by faith" (Rom 1:17). Abraham was set right with God because he committed himself to God, believing his promise that he would be blessed. His right relationship with God is not established once and for all; rather, it must be continued through his life. Therefore, ultimately, the issue is not about how one achieves a new legal status but how to live faithfully to God.

---

4. Frank Matera also sees this *pistis christou* as a subjective genitive. See Matera, *Galatians*, 92.

5. The old version of NIV 1984 reflects this interpretation: "A righteousness comes from God . . ." (Rom 3:22).

Regarding the second issue, "how to be set right with God," the typical interpretation is, as noted before, one can be justified once and for all likely in a legal court. Jesus solved the problem of sins and what believers need is to accept his salvific work. Jesus was punished in place of sinners or he paid for the price of sins. Likewise, Jesus offered himself as a perfect sacrifice and replaced the old covenant and its sacrificial system. The law is imperfect and outdated, and it is not a perfect means of justification. The only way of justification is faith in Christ. Here, faith is understood narrowly as the knowledge that Jesus solved all problems of sins. Then, their justification is done once and for all. But the above traditional view of forensic salvation is problematic because faith is more than knowledge; it is a *commitment* to God or to Christ. When one has faith, one must trust God and follow Jesus. As Jesus was faithful to God, who also is faithful toward humanity, Jesus's followers must also be faithful to God, dying with Christ and following in his footsteps.

Therefore, even if we say justification is by faith in Christ, this faith is not a type of knowledge, a belief in the truth of certain propositions, but the "faith *working through love*" (Gal 5:6) or seeking the love of neighbor (Gal 5:14; Rom 13:8–10). When God considers Abraham righteous in the story of Gen 15:6, he does not mean that Abraham's legal status has changed to a righteous person, but he means that Abraham did a good job, trusting his promise. Namely, God recognizes his faith and commends him. Faith is an expression of trust that requires holistic commitment in one's life, and because of that trust, Abraham had to walk his faith through the ups and downs until his death. His faith journey was not always smooth, but he endured, whether in good or bad times. Faith is not mere belief *about* God or Jesus. Rather, it compels one to devote one's life to the cause of God and of Jesus, which involves proclaiming the gospel of God through Jesus. In sum, one can be set right with God through faith, but this faith is not the knowledge or confession that Jesus is the Savior who solved the problem of sins. The true faith is that which works through love.

Justification

Dikaiosynē is translated into righteousness or justification. When it is used of God, it may mean God's character, such as righteousness, steadfast love, and justice. When the verbal form of *dikaioō* is used with persons (for example in Gal 2:16), the meaning is a bit complex. The verb means various things, according to context;

---

for example, to put into a right relationship with God, to declare as righteous, to prove to be right, to set free, or to acknowledge God's justice.[6] In Gal 2:16, *dikaioutai* (third person, singular, present, passive, indicative of *dikaioō*) is used and the verse is usually translated from the perspective of forensic salvation with the imagery of a legal court. Likewise, usually, *pistis christou* is translated as an objective genitive, rendering it believer's faith in Christ. So the New Revised Standard Version goes like this: "yet we know that a person is *justified not by the works of the law but through faith in Jesus Christ*. And we have come to believe in Christ Jesus, so that we might be *justified by faith in Christ*, and not by doing the works of the law, because no one will be *justified by the works of the law*." But this translation does not convey well what Paul may mean in this context. Paul's point is a holistic relationship with God. So a better translation may be: "a person is set right with God . . ." In other words, the issue is whether one has a good relationship with God. Furthermore, *pistis christou* must be a subjective genitive ("Christ's faithfulness"), which makes better sense, as we will see in this book.

Regarding the third issue, "how to interpret *pistis christou*," we have to ask whose faith is involved here in *pistis christou*. As we saw before, traditionally, *pistis christou* has been interpreted as "faith in Christ" (as an objective genitive). Here, Christ is the object of faith. In this view, Christ completed the salvific work by dying instead of sinners. Sins are cleansed and sinners are granted righteousness if they have faith in Christ; they are justified once and for all. But even in this objective genitive, faith may be understood differently, as noted before: faith as trusting God and following Christ. Understood this way, faith in Christ can be very ethical and good because believers participate in Christ's life and death.

But the question is: Does Paul here really talk about believer's faith in Christ? Or, does he care about Christ's faithfulness? *Pistis christou* is more likely a subjective genitive: "Christ's faithfulness." As "the faith of Abraham" in Rom 4:16 is understood as Abraham's faith(fulness), "the faith of Christ" must be Christ's faithfulness, as seen in the following: Gal 2:16, 20; 3:22; Phil 3:9; Rom 3:22, 26. The big difference from the objective genitive reading is that now Christ is the subject of faith or faithfulness. That is, Paul talks about Christ's faithfulness, which must be the basis of Christian faith.

6. *BibleWorks* (Bible software).

This faithfulness of Christ can be understood in relation to God, who is also faithful. Paul is familiar with the view that God is faithful in the Hebrew Scriptures (cf. Isa 49:7). God calls Abraham, who was a nobody at that time, gives him hope, and makes a covenant with him (Gen 12–15). Paul describes God as the faithful, righteous one, who is the source of the gospel (cf. Rom 1:1, 17; 3:3; 1 Cor 1:9; Gal 3:8). In 1 Thess 5:24, God is said to be faithful and he will keep his people safe and sanctify them: "The one who calls you is faithful, and he will do this." In 1 Cor 1:9, the Corinthians were called by the faithful God: "God is faithful; by him you were called into the fellowship of his Son, Jesus Christ our Lord." God called them into the fellowship of his Son. In 1 Cor 10:13, God is faithful because he will take care of his people in times of trouble: "No testing has overtaken you that is not common to everyone. God is faithful, and he will not let you be tested beyond your strength, but with the testing he will also provide the way out so that you may be able to endure it." The last example of God's faithfulness in Paul's undisputed letters is in 2 Cor 1:18: "As surely as God is faithful, our word to you has not been 'Yes and No.'" In the above, we saw a few examples in his texts that Paul specifies that God is faithful.

As God is faithful, Christ is also faithful. This theme of Christ's faithfulness is prevalent in Paul's undisputed letters. Let us take a few examples. In Rom 1:1–3, Christ is described as the Son of God who carried out God's good news. God promised the good news beforehand "through his prophets in the holy scriptures" (Rom 1:2). This means God is faithful and caring for his people. Then, this gospel of God concerns his Son (Rom 1:3), who was faithful to God and did not spare his life for God's righteousness (cf. Rom 3:21–26; 5:12–21; Phil 2:6–11; Gal 2:16; 3:22). Jesus as the Son of God exemplified God's love and his righteousness in the world. He was crucified because of his work of God, but God raised him from the dead (Rom 1:4). This work of Jesus brings the good news of God down to earth. That is the gospel of Christ, which Paul says he is eager to proclaim: "For God, whom I serve with my spirit by announcing the gospel of his Son, is my witness that without ceasing I remember you always in my prayers" (Rom 1:9).

In Galatians also, the theme of Christ's faithfulness is observed, and we saw this when we dealt with Gal 1:4 and 1:7. In Gal 1:4, Christ is the one "who gave himself for our sins to set us free from the present evil age, according to the will of our God and Father."[7] In Gal 1:7, Paul says there are some who "pervert the gospel of Christ." We interpreted Christ's giving of

---

7. Martyn, *Galatians*, 271. He emphasizes Christ's faithful death and his faith.

himself as a moral sacrifice to help his followers to live a life of freedom (cf. 1 Cor 15:3; 2 Cor 5:21; Rom 5:6–10; 8:3–4; Mark 10:45). Jesus's sacrifice is a moral example that he faithfully demonstrated God's righteousness. What he did for God and the world shows his faithfulness to God. As we saw in Gal 1:1–10, "the gospel of Christ" has to do with what he did for God and the world (cf. 1 Thess 3:2; 1 Cor 9:12; Phil 1:27). As we will see later in Gal 2:20, Paul says he wants to live by the faith of Jesus.

Because Christ is faithful, his followers are also to be faithful. They "have received grace and apostleship through Jesus," and their purpose is "to bring about the obedience of faith among all the gentiles for the sake of his name" (Rom 1:5). As Jesus was obedient to God, revealing God's love and his righteousness, his followers are commissioned to do the same, so that all the gentiles may come to the same faith of Jesus. Paul says that the righteous one will live by faith (Rom 1:17) and that God will justify those who have the faith of Jesus (Rom 3:26). In other words, those who share the faith of Jesus and follow him are the righteous people. Christians' faithfulness must be based on Christ's faithfulness. This idea in Romans is also seen in Gal 2:16 where the basis of Christian faithfulness requires the faithfulness of Christ (*pistis christou*).[8] That is, one is set right with God through the faithfulness of Jesus Christ. This means "we have come to *believe into* Christ Jesus" (*pisteuō eis*). The preposition *eis* ("into") indicates Christians' participation in Christ. One's right relationship with God needs Christ's faithfulness, which means one has to participate in his faithfulness. Thus far we have seen three aspects of faith: God's faithfulness, Christ Jesus's faithfulness, and Christians' faithfulness. These three are related to one another. God is on top of this relationship and Christ is a true respondent to God's faithfulness. As a result, his followers receive grace and apostleship through him. Therefore, if we miss Christ's faithfulness and his moral sacrifice, we miss the truth of the gospel.

8. See Richard Longenecker, *Galatians*, 87, 145. See also Bruce Longenecker, *The Triumph of Abraham's God*, 103–16.

Faith

The concept of faith in the Hebrew Bible concerns trust, as Hebrew *emunah* connotes.[9] Indeed, in it, God is the most faithful character. Because God is faithful and steadfast, his people also have to be faithful to him. This means "the righteous one will live by faith" (Hab 2:4). Faith and righteousness are never two separate things. The righteous person is the faithful one. In the Roman world, Latin *fides* comes close to faith and its basic meaning is also trust or loyalty. In Greek, *pistis* also means basically trust. When this word is used in the New Testament, its meaning is diverse and divergent. The verb of *pistis* is *pisteuō* and is used frequently in the Gospels. Its basic meaning is to trust. Jesus trusts God and proclaims the good news of God. His followers are expected to show the same trust to God. In Paul's undisputed letters, Paul talks about faith in a threefold way: God's faithfulness; Christ's faithfulness; and Christians' faithfulness. God is faithful (1 Cor 1:9). Christ is faithful to God and demonstrated God's righteousness through faithfulness (Rom 3:22). Christians' faithfulness means to imitate Christ. God justifies those who have the faithfulness of Jesus (Rom 3:26). But when it comes to Deutero-Pauline and Pastoral Letters, the concept of faith changes. Mostly, faith means a set of knowledge; it is mainly about Jesus and his salvific death. Thus "faith in Christ" (*pistis en christō*), not *pistis christou* (genitive case), appears in the Deutero-Pauline and Pastoral Letters (Col 1:4; 2 Tim 3:15).[10] In Hebrews, we see a still different concept of faith, which has more to do with assurance or conviction about the future. In James, faith is expressed differently but is not different from Paul. James emphasizes faith and works together because some say faith without works is valid. Paul's concept of faith includes works (deeds). He never separates faith from works. The righteous person will live by faith (Rom 1:17).

Regarding the last issue, "how to interpret 'the works of the law,'" Paul says one is not set right with God through "the works of the law," which refer to specific Jewish laws or regulations about circumcision, food, or purity. Earlier in Gal 2:1–10, he pointed out the primacy of the gospel through faith at the Council of Jerusalem, and in Gal 2:11–14, he challenged Peter's hypocritical position about the gospel. Here in Gal 2:16, he makes clear

---

9. Kim, *A Theological Introduction to Paul's Letters*, 64.
10. Kim, *Preaching the New Testament Again*, 27–28.

that one is set right with God through faith, not by the works of the law. His point is faith comes before the law. If one is faithful, he/she must keep the law, loving God and neighbor. What is at stake is a matter of priority or balance between faith and the law. Otherwise, he does not reject the law per se or works of the law themselves. In Paul's thinking, as he pointed out, Abraham's faith is the starting point for a good, righteous life; faith precedes the law. Nevertheless, the law is holy (Rom 7:12). He also makes it clear that faith does not nullify the law; rather, the law is upheld through faith (Rom 3:31). Put differently, faith informs the law, and the purpose/summary of the law is the love of neighbor, as in Gal 5:14: "The whole law is summed up in a single commandment: 'You shall love your neighbor as yourself.'"

Faith and Works

In Paul's thinking, faith and works are not juxtaposed with each other if "works" means deeds. To have faith means to trust God and Jesus, and at the same time, faith means to participate in Christ's faithfulness. As he quotes from Hab 2:4, the righteous one has to *live by faith*. "To live by faith" means faith and works are inseparable. In this regard, Paul's view of faith is the same as James 2:26: "For just as the body without the spirit is dead, so faith without works is also dead." In Gal 2:16, Paul opposes "the works *of the law*," which are most likely Jewish-specific laws and practice, such as circumcision or food laws, that are wrongly imposed onto the gentiles.

With this view of faith, he responds to the circumcision faction, saying, "We are Jews by birth, . . . yet we know that a person is set right with God not by the works of the law but through faith" (Gal 2:15–16). While "the works of the law" may be good for Christian Jews, it cannot be imposed on the gentile Christians because it is not essential to them. For example, circumcision may be good for Christian Jews if they stay in faith. But for gentile Christians, while the law is good, not every piece of the law can be kept as Jews keep them. Rather, gentile believers reinterpret the law through faith and keep it with a focus on the love of God and the love of neighbor. Especially, Paul emphasizes the latter because the love of God is included in the latter. So, he says: "For in Christ Jesus neither circumcision nor uncircumcision counts for anything; the only thing that counts is faith working through love" (Gal 5:6).

Consider and discuss: *Pistis christou* in Gal 2:16 may be translated in two different ways: "faith in Christ" (objective genitive) and "Christ's faithfulness" (subjective genitive). Which makes better sense and why?

In Gal 2:17–18, Paul asks a rhetorical question about justification in Christ: "But if, while seeking to be set right with God in Christ, we ourselves have been found to be sinners, is Christ then a servant of sin? Certainly not!" Here "justification in Christ" means one's good relationship with God, which is done in Christ. "In Christ" here is a modal dative that tells of Christians' attitude and behavior matching the way of Christ. In other words, one can be set right with God through the way of Christ. This idea of justification was stated in 2:16: "One is justified not by the works of the law, but through the faithfulness of Christ Jesus." "Through the faithfulness of Jesus" connotes Christian participation in Christ. All this implies that the followers of Jesus have to make intentional efforts in following Jesus, changing their life and mind toward the way of Christ. In this process of having a new, good relationship with God through Christ, one is deeply aware of one's sinfulness and weakness. But this does not mean that Christ is a servant of sin in the sense that he promotes sin. In other words, Paul's point is that sin is not promoted or taken for granted even if Christians receive grace and turn to God through Christ. There may have been some misunderstanding about the grace and sin in the churches of Galatia as we saw in the Roman churches (Rom 5:20—6:3). Some Christians thought that the more sins they commit, the more grace they receive. They were morally dead and did not see the seriousness of sin or evil; instead, they naively believed in the grace of God. In a sense, God's grace is always available for anyone who comes to him through Christ. But once they turned to God by the grace of God, they should not sin but try to live in Christ as much as they can, putting to death the deeds of the body by the Spirit (Rom 8:13). So Paul disavows the idea of "the more sin, the more grace" in Rom 6:1–3: "What then are we to say? Should we continue in sin in order that grace may abound? By no means! How can we who died to sin go on living in it? Do you not know that all of us who have been baptized into Christ Jesus were baptized into his death?" Therefore, Paul's response to the Galatians is while sin is exposed and named in the process of one's justification with God, it cannot be repeated as if grace would cover it. If it is repeated, one is a transgressor. Thus, Paul says in Gal 2:18, "But if I build up again the very things that I once tore down, then I demonstrate that I am a transgressor."

In Gal 2:19, Paul clarifies about the law: "For through the law I died to the law, so that I might live to God. I have been crucified with Christ." Since the law was given by God, it should be interpreted from the perspective of God. In other words, people should know what God wants when the law was given. The law has many functions: helping them to stay in a covenantal community; guiding and protecting them; disciplining them; establishing justice in society. All of these laws can be summarized in the love of neighbor (Gal 5:14; Rom 13:8–10). All works of the law should be helpful in embracing the love of neighbor. Otherwise, works of the law without love are harmful to the community.

With the above understanding of the law, "dying to the law" means one should not live to the law when it is not understood as centered on God or on the love of neighbor. In other words, one must live to God through faith. Then the law will be upheld. That is, while the law is good and holy, it did not produce the expected result, not because it is imperfect, but because humans are evil, seeking their glory and power. Thus God sent his own Son, who experienced weakness, persecution, and even death in his faithfulness to God. That is, he demonstrated God's righteousness and fulfilled the love of neighbor through faith. So Paul does not say that the law is inferior to faith (Rom 3:31; 7.12). The law to which one has to die signifies one's narrow interpretation of the law without the love of neighbor. Many observant Jews may think they love God because they keep the law strictly. But the question is, What if there is no love of neighbor? Does God want *that* kind of law keeping? Thus, Paul says in Gal 2:19: "For through the law I died to the law, so that I might live to God." "Through the law" can be interpreted through the way of Christ or the way Christ lived, which also has to do with "the gospel of Christ" (Gal 1:7; cf. Gal 1:4). "Through the law" means the way that Christ fulfilled the law (Gal 3:24; Rom 10:4). Namely, in 1:4, he gave himself for freedom of the people and loved them. His love of God and neighbor is the summary of the law. As a result, the followers of Jesus may live by faith that upholds the law. They also have to bear one another's burden because in this way they will fulfill "the law of Christ" (Gal 6:2). The law of Christ is the way Christ lived. Also, in Rom 7:4, Paul echoes a similar idea about dying to the law: "In the same way, my friends, you have died to the law *through the body of Christ*, so that you may belong to another, to him who has been raised from the dead in order that we may bear fruit for

God." Here, "through the body of Christ" implies Christ's crucifixion or his faithfulness to God.

In sum, when one has died to the law through the way of Christ, one can live to God. This means one can seek God's righteousness and justice in society. Therefore, Paul says finally in Gal 2:19, "I have been crucified with Christ," which means a full commitment to his living the way of Christ. He does not live simply by the law but through faith working through love, through the way of Christ.

In the end, in Gal 2:20, Paul expresses his confession about Christ and his determination to live by Christ's faithfulness. In Gal 2:20, he says, "and it is no longer I who live, but it is Christ who lives in me. And the life I now live in the flesh I live *by the faith of the Son of God*, who loved me and gave himself for me" (my translation; italics for emphasis). Paul's logic is this: Since he has been crucified with Christ, there is no self that lives in him. In other words, the living subject is not he but Christ. Therefore, Christ must rule him. Thus, he says he wants to live by the faithfulness of the Son of God, not by his faith in the Son of God (an objective genitive). Christ is everything to him because he did not spare his life, loving him, so he needs to imitate him and follow his faith.

Galatians 2:21 concludes the section, Gal 2:11–21, and it reads: "I do not nullify the grace of God; for if justification comes through the law, then Christ died for nothing." First of all, Paul clarifies the gospel by the grace of God. In other words, the good news comes from God and is based on God's grace. Without God's grace, there would be no Abraham to be called. One's relationship with God would be impossible without it. Paul always looks to God's grace and his promise of blessings to humanity. In terms of the order, God's grace comes first, and then faith follows. The law was given after that and therefore, it should be interpreted through the faith that seeks to trust God and love neighbor.

This is why Paul says, "For if justification comes through the law, then Christ died for nothing." "Justification coming through the law" means one thinks that one is made righteous simply by depending on the law with zeal apart from faith. But Jesus does not agree to that idea, and he was crucified because of that. He clarified the law with a focus on the love of neighbor, and he was crucified because of his radical love of God and neighbor by breaking or reinterpreting the law. His crucifixion is the result of his faithful obedience to the good news of God that must expand to the poor and oppressed. If Jesus had supported a traditional interpretation of the Jewish law, he would not have been crucified. Paul's point is the law can never be the first. Faith is that which can uphold the law, and this faith is to trust God and follow Jesus who fulfilled the law through faith. Otherwise, Paul never says that the law is simply bad or imperfect. Even if his view of the law sounds very negative, it must be understood within the context of the situation in the Galatian church, where some were teaching that the law or "the works of the law" are to be considered absolute before faith.

SECTION IV

3:1–29

The Root of the Gospel

IN THE PREVIOUS SECTION (Gal 2:1–21), we saw the clarification of the gospel in relation to Jewish law and culture. In Gal 3:1–19, Paul traces back to the root of the gospel in the story of Abraham. The root of the gospel is God's promise to Abraham that *all people* will be blessed in him, which means that they will follow his faith (Gal 3:8; cf. Gen 12:3). Abraham believed God's good news and his promise. This good news of God, promised to Abraham, was realized through Jesus's faithfulness for all who have faith.

Chiasm in Gal 3:1–29

Galatians 3:1–29 involves a chiasm (*A, B, C, D, C', B', A'*) that helps us understand the root of the gospel.

  A 3:1–5 Confusion in the church due to the lack of faith
    B 3:6–12 The gospel through Abraham's faith
      C 3:13–16 Receiving the promise of the Spirit through Christ
        D 3:17–18 The gospel rooted in God's promise
      C' 3:19–21 God's promises do not depend on the law
    B' 3:22–25 The gospel through Jesus Christ's faithfulness
  A' 3:26–29 A new vision of the community in Christ

A (3:1–5), "Confusion in the church due to the lack of faith," is contrasted with *A'* (3:26–29), "A new vision of a community in Christ." In the former,

53

the churches of Galatia are disunited and confused due to the lack of faith, and in the latter, there is a new vision of the community in Christ. *B* (3:6–12), "The gospel through Abraham's faith," is paired with *B'* (3:22–25), "The gospel through Jesus Christ's faithfulness." In the former, Abraham faithfully responds to God's good news, and in the latter, Jesus also responds to the promise of God through faith. Then, *C* (3:13–16), "Receiving the promise of the Spirit through Christ," is explained with *C'* (3:19–21), "God's promises do not depend on the law." In the former, the promise of the Spirit is received through faith, and in the latter, God's promises do not depend on the law. *D* (3:17–18) is the central unit: "The gospel through God's promise." That is, the gospel is rooted in God's promise.

Good News or Gospel

Greek *euangelion* means "good news." This term does not directly refer to the four canonical Gospels. What good news means depends on the context and content of it. The Roman Emperor proclaims the good news about his birth or victory in war. There are also notions of the good news in the Hebrew Bible. Prophets bring good news about God's justice to Israelites. At other times, they deliver messages of hope and protection to the exiles in Babylon. Overall in the Hebrew Bible, the good news is from God and it is also about God, who promises good things to Abraham and his descendants. God is pictured as a faithful, righteous, sovereign, one who must rule the earth with justice and love. Now in the New Testament, there are various notions of the good news.

In the Synoptic Gospels, basically, the good news is about God, to whom Jesus testifies. So the good news is about God's reign (*basileia tou theou*, Mark 1:14–15; Luke 8:1; Matt 4:17–23, 43). Jesus proclaimed the good news of God and says in Mark 1:15: "The time is fulfilled, and the kingdom of God has come near; repent, and believe in the good news." Jesus taught that now is God's time that people have to change their minds and seek God's will. He also cured the sick and challenged the system of evil. Jesus's message of God's reign is against Rome's rule. So there are political ramifications that eventually cost his life.

John's Gospel does not explicitly use the term, but that does not mean there is no "good news" in it. Jesus's testimony to God and his work of God bring light and life to the world full of darkness and evil. He embodies the Logos of God whose purpose is to make the world a place of love (John 3:16). His followers have to accept and trust him, and then they may live abundantly in the Spirit. That is good news.

When it comes to Paul's undisputed letters, Paul elaborates on the good news and talks about the threefold gospel: "the good news of God" (Rom 1:1; 15:16; 1 Thess 2:2, 8–9), "the good news of Christ" (Gal 1:7; 1 Cor 9:2; 2 Cor 9:13; Phil 1:27; 1 Thess 3:2), and the good news he proclaims (Romans and Galatians as a whole may be understood as Paul's gospel). Paul's major difference with the Gospels is he articulates the gospel in a threefold manner. First, the good news is *about God*, which is the same as the Gospels. Second, he also talks about "the good news *of Christ*," which is an added element. The good news of Christ can be understood in two ways. One, it may be the good news that Jesus proclaimed. In other words, we have to see what he did for God and the world. Two, it may be also good news about him. This is because he did great things for God and the world. Lastly, the good news must continue to spread through the *proclamation* of Jesus's followers.

When it comes to Deutero-Pauline and Pastoral Letters, the concept of good news changes. It is basically understood as a set of teachings about Jesus who completed salvation. There is no articulation about the good news of God. The whole emphasis is the gospel about Jesus. The gospel is salvific knowledge that people have to acknowledge and believe. Such belief is so much so that there is no emphasis on Christ's faith or Christians' participation in his faithfulness.

A 3:1-5 CONFUSION IN THE CHURCH DUE TO THE LACK OF FAITH

1 You foolish Galatians! Who has bewitched you? It was before your eyes that Jesus Christ was publicly exhibited as crucified! 2 The only thing I want to learn from you is this: Did you receive the Spirit by doing the works of the law or by believing what you heard? 3 Are you so foolish? Having started with the Spirit, are you now ending with the flesh? 4 Did you experience so much for nothing?—if it really was for nothing. 5 Well then, does God supply you with the Spirit and work miracles among you by your doing the works of the law, or by your believing what you heard?

In Gal 3:1, Paul says: "You foolish Galatians! Who has bewitched you? It was before your eyes that Jesus Christ was publicly exhibited as crucified!" Here "You foolish Galatians" does not mean that all Galatians are foolish or irrational. He addresses all of them collectively because he is concerned with the whole community. There are some who are confusing them and want to pervert the gospel of Christ (Gal 1:7). These people are from the circumcision faction. They are irrational (*anoetos*), which means they do not understand "the gospel of Christ." Then, he asks: "Who has bewitched you?" He probably refers to certain people who came from James (Gal 2:11–14). Given the activity of false believers who were brought to the apostolic council at Jerusalem, James's people or the circumcision faction must have been very influential to many Galatians.

Then Paul reminds the Galatians of Jesus's crucifixion and the significance of the gospel of Christ crucified: "It was before your eyes that Jesus Christ was publicly exhibited as crucified!" Paul's proclamation of the gospel is not only about God but also about Christ crucified (cf. 1 Cor 1:23; 2:2). Christ crucified evokes many images of his work: his innocent prophetic death, his love of God, his love of the oppressed and marginalized, and his sacrifice for God's righteousness. For Paul, Christ was crucified because of all of these.[1] Through his faithfulness he revealed who God is and what God wants (cf. Rom 3:22). His death is neither to pay for the debt of sin nor is it needed in any sense of the traditional atonement theories. It is the cost of his proclamation of the gospel of God.

In fact, throughout his letters, Paul emphasizes Christ crucified. In 1 Cor 1:23, Paul says: "but we proclaim Christ crucified, a stumbling block to Jews and foolishness to gentiles." Jesus's crucifixion must be a sign of failure as a messiah for Jews. For them, the Messiah will not be hung on a tree; rather, he must show power to the world and liberate Israel from the oppression of Rome. Thus, Jesus's crucifixion is a stumbling block to Jews. To the gentile world, it is considered foolish because people want success, fame, power, and status. But Paul says he proclaims Christ crucified, saying, "For I decided to know nothing among you except Jesus Christ, and him crucified" (1 Cor 2:2). In Galatians as well, he draws on this image of Christ crucified indirectly and directly. For example, in Gal 1:4, Jesus "gave himself for our sins to set us free from the present evil age, according to the will of our God and Father." Also in Gal 1:6, Paul says he is astonished that some people quickly desert God, who called them in the grace of Christ,

---

1. See Kim, *Messiah in Weakness*, 106–18.

and that they are turning to a different gospel, which may be both a form of the Jewish version of the gospel and various forms of preaching about Christ, not based on Christ crucified. Paul says in Gal 1:7 that "there are some who are confusing you and want to pervert the gospel of Christ." In Gal 2:19 he says, "I have been crucified with Christ." Gal 5:24 says: "And those who belong to Christ Jesus have crucified the flesh with its passions and desires." Galatians 6:14 says, "May I never boast of anything except the cross of our Lord Jesus Christ, by which the world has been crucified to me, and I to the world."

Then, what is the meaning of Christ crucified to Paul and the Galatians? For Paul, Christ crucified—not Christ raised—is the foundation of the church.[2] While the church (*ekklesia*) belongs to God, its foundation is Christ crucified because Jesus "gave himself for our sins to set us free from the present evil age, according to the will of our God and Father" (Gal 1:4; cf. Rom 5:6–8; 8:2–3). In other words, the foundation of the church is Jesus's love of people (Gal 1:6; 2:20) and his faithfulness to God (cf. Rom 3:21–26; 5:12–21; Phil 2:6–11; Gal 2:16; 3:22).

> **Consider and discuss:** In Paul's theology, he emphasizes Christ crucified. Why is it important to his gospel? Some think that the center or his theology is Jesus's resurrection. Do you agree? If not, how can you relate his crucifixion to resurrection?

Christ crucified is more than theology for Paul. He experienced physical weaknesses due to illness and underwent hardships due to his work for Christ. Whenever he felt weary, weak, and hopeless, he remembered Christ's faithfulness to God and his love of him (2:20). Then he could regain energy and strength from the Spirit. More than this, he even confesses that he became strong through his experience of difficulties in his life: "but he [the Lord] said to me, 'My grace is sufficient for you, for power is made perfect in weakness.' So, I will boast all the more gladly of my weaknesses, so that the power of Christ may dwell in me" (2 Cor 12:9).

---

2. In Paul's theological thinking, the resurrection of Jesus is not the most important event. The most significant part of Jesus's life is his faithfulness and sacrifice for God's righteousness. He was crucified because of this work. Resurrection is God's way of dealing with evil. In this regard, Alain Badiou's emphasis on the resurrection of Jesus does not make sense. He considers that the most important event about Jesus is the resurrection of Jesus. He argues that we have to learn Paul's universalism based on the love and resurrection of Jesus. Badiou, *St. Paul: The Foundation of Universalism*, 65–97.

In this regard, Paul's experience and theology about God and Christ were different from other typical Christian leaders or Jerusalem apostles. He was a diaspora Jew who accepted Jesus as the Jewish Messiah for all. But his credentials were not well accepted among Christians and the gentiles, especially in Jerusalem and throughout the Jewish diaspora communities. But he realized that his weaknesses were incomparable to Jesus because Jesus gave himself for him and others. Thus he says in 2 Cor 12:10, "Therefore I am content with weaknesses, insults, hardships, persecutions, and calamities for the sake of Christ; for whenever I am weak, then I am strong." With this above view of Christ crucified to the church, Paul asks the Galatians, "How can you forget the image of Christ crucified in your life? How can you desert the one who called you in the grace of Jesus Christ? How can you forget Christ's love of you?"

In Gal 3:2–5, Paul asks a series of rhetorical questions and reminds the Galatians of their time of receiving the Spirit through faith, contrasting it with the present time in which they stick to the works of the law:

> 2 The only thing I want to learn from you is this: Did you receive the Spirit by doing the works of the law or by believing what you heard? 3 Are you so foolish? Having started with the Spirit, are you now ending with the flesh? 4 Did you experience so much for nothing?—if it really was for nothing. 5 Well then, does God supply you with the Spirit and work miracles among you by your doing the works of the law, or by your believing what you heard?

In the above passage, Paul says the Spirit has come to the Galatians because they believed what they heard.[3] They heard about God and Jesus— the grace of God and the faithfulness of Jesus. They accepted the love of God through the grace of Jesus (Gal 1:6). What they heard is good things about God: God is the good news, hope, rock, redeemer, and salvation. They also heard good things about Jesus, God's Son, who proclaimed the good news of God and gave himself for them. So the Galatians accepted this gospel through Paul and they were pleased. But some of them were confused about the gospel and did not follow the work of the Spirit. They sought to be justified by doing the works of the law. But Paul's argument is this: The Spirit came to them when they responded to God who called

---

3. The Spirit appears throughout Galatians: 3:14; 4:6, 29; 5:16–18; 22–23, 25; 6:1, 8. The Spirit as God's Spirit has many roles to play for Christians: for example, helping them believe what they heard; exhorting them to live by faith; comforting them in times of trouble or suffering.

them in the grace of Christ, and it did not come by doing the works of the law, such as practicing particular laws or regulations such as circumcision or dietary laws.

B 3:6–12 THE GOSPEL THROUGH ABRAHAM'S FAITH

6 Just as Abraham "believed God, and it was reckoned to him as righteousness," 7 so, you see, those who believe are the descendants of Abraham. 8 And the scripture, foreseeing that God would justify the gentiles by faith, declared the gospel beforehand to Abraham, saying, "All the gentiles [or nations (*ethnē*)] shall be blessed in you." 9 For this reason, those who believe are blessed with Abraham who believed. 10 For all who rely on the works of the law are under a curse; for it is written, "Cursed is everyone who does not observe and obey all the things written in the book of the law." 11 Now it is evident that no one is justified before God by the law; for "The one who is righteous will live by faith." 12 But the law does not rest on faith; on the contrary, "Whoever does the works of the law will live by them."

In Gal 3:6–12, Paul traces faith to Abraham's story and argues that the gospel came through his faith, not by doing "the works of the law." First of all, in Gal 3:6, he cites Gen 15:6, which says that Abraham believed God when he heard he would be blessed with numerous descendants. This is not the only time he believed in God. In fact, since God called him, he continued to live by faith during his life, though his faith was not perfect. He left his home and kindred according to God's command. But his faith journey was not going well. In a hopeless situation, he heard God's blessings of descendants and he believed. Here, the verb "to believe" comes from *emunah* in Hebrew, which means faithfulness or steadfastness. Abraham's faith is more than his agreement to God's blessing or his promises. It means his commitment to God and his persistent hope in the God-given future.[4] Then, God considered his faithfulness as righteousness, which means he is commendable. Abraham's faithfulness is a merit that God acknowledges.

Then, in Gal 3:7, Paul says that "those who believe are the descendants of Abraham." In Genesis and elsewhere in the Hebrew Bible, Abraham's descendants are understood as all who come through his lineage. All the descendants of Abraham are meant to live by faith just like their common

4. Kim, "Between Text and Sermon: Hebrews 11:8–16," 204–6.

ancestor Abraham. At this point, Paul extends God's covenant with Abraham to all who believe. His argument is this: "Those who believe are the descendants of Abraham." As Abraham was called by God and received God's blessing by faith, whoever comes to God by faith would be accepted as a child of God.

Paul goes on to say in Gal 3:8, "And the scripture, foreseeing that God would justify the gentiles by faith, declared the gospel beforehand to Abraham, saying, 'All the gentiles shall be blessed in you.'" First of all, this scriptural saying echoes Gen 12:3: "All the families of the earth shall be blessed in you." In Paul's time, many Jews considered only themselves the true descendants of Abraham. As covenant beneficiaries, they keep the law to stay in a covenantal community. They also believe that the whole world ("all the families of the earth") will be blessed through the way of Judaism, which means people have to keep the laws. But Paul thinks differently, that the descendants of Abraham are not defined by the law or by doing the works of the law, but through faith. This faith is one's persistent faithfulness towards God and unending hope in the future.

As Abraham believed in God and his promise to him, all the gentiles (or all nations) can follow his example and be blessed in him.[5] So Paul says the scripture declared the gospel beforehand to Abraham. This gospel is none other than what Abraham heard from God about his future. The gospel is not a new concept made by Jesus or Paul. It is God's good news that all people will be blessed through faith. Paul even says the scripture foresaw that "God would justify the gentiles by faith." When Abraham was called, he was not a Jew or an Israelite; indeed, such a concept did not exist. But through Abraham's responding faith to God, he became a seed of blessing to all who come to God through the same kind of faith, which is to trust God wholeheartedly. Then, in Gal 3:9, Paul offers a conclusion: "For this reason, those who believe are blessed with Abraham who believed."

In Gal 3:10–12, Paul explains why those who rely on the works of the law are not set right with God. We have to be careful to bear in mind the context in Galatia where "the works of the law" were being absolutized at the expense of faith. Otherwise, Paul does not simply reject the Jewish law or the works of the law. The issue is a matter of balance or, better, priority. Faith does not and cannot overthrow the law because the law was given by God (Rom 3:31; 7:12). Moreover, Paul believes the law can be

---

5. The Greek word *ethnē* means the gentiles or nations, which indicates all peoples of the earth.

upheld through faith. The problem is to *rely* on the works of the law, which means not to depend on faith. In Paul's view, faith comes *before* the law, and God's promise or call comes before faith. Therefore, those who rely on the works of the law ignore God. Faith is to hear and trust God. A faithful person stands on God's side and does what is required as a child of God, loving God and neighbor. Faith also means total dependence on God and his providential care. Fear has no place before faith. But if anyone lives by *relying* on the law (or doing the works of the law without faith) he or she is under a curse because there is no grace of God. Moreover, the truth is that no one is perfect with the law. So Paul says: "Cursed is everyone who does not observe and obey all the things written in the book of the law" (Gal 3:10, quoted from Deut 27:26). He also says in 3:11 that "Now it is evident that no one is justified before God by the law; for 'The one who is righteous will live by faith'" (quoted from Hab 2:4). The righteous person is the one who lives by faith, which means he or she should be faithful to God and have to live continuously through faith.

In Gal 3:12, Paul goes on to explain why the law does not rest on faith. The reason is: "Whoever does the works of the law will live by them," which refers to "all who rely on the works of the law" (Gal 3:10). Again, we must be careful that here the law needs to be understood within the context of the Galatian situation where specific works of the law such as the circumcision or dietary regulations are an issue. The problem is not the law itself but some people (for example, "James's people" or the circumcision faction) who *replace* faith by the law or by the works of the law. Those who rely on the works of the law do not depend on God or his promise. In this sense, Paul says that "the law does not rest on faith." The real issue is whether one can live by faith or not. If one is faithful, the law can be discerned and summarized with the love of neighbor, as Paul does so in Gal 5:14. Similarly, for Paul, what matters is faith working through love.

C 3:13-16 RECEIVING THE PROMISE OF THE SPIRIT THROUGH CHRIST

> 13 Christ redeemed us from the curse of the law by becoming a curse for us—for it is written, "Cursed is everyone who hangs on a tree"— 14 in order that in Christ Jesus the blessing of Abraham might come to the gentiles, so that we might receive the promise of the Spirit through faith. 15 Brothers and sisters, I give an example

from daily life: once a person's will has been ratified, no one adds to it or annuls it. 16 Now the promises were made to Abraham and to his offspring; it does not say, "And to offsprings," as of many; but it says, "And to your offspring," that is, to one person, who is Christ.

In Gal 3:13, Paul states that "Christ redeemed us from the curse of the law by becoming a curse for us." The critical issue here is how to understand "the curse of the law" and Christ's redemption of people. The curse of the law should not be understood from an old perspective in which faith in Christ replaces the law, which is considered an imperfect means of justification because no one can keep it perfectly. This view does not hold true because Paul has never rejected the law (cf. Rom 3:31). We can explain the law's curse from the context of Galatians. The main issue in the churches of Galatia has to do with the circumcision faction or James's people who push the gentile Galatians to follow Jewish laws. These people have a zeal for the law in addition to faith. Then their relying on the law makes them move away from the faith. They are judged and ruled by the law. Since they are "under the law," there is no freedom that comes through faith. Therefore, the law without faith can be a curse for them. But Christ Jesus discerned the law and fulfilled it through faith (cf. Rom 10:4). He was not ruled by the law nor under it, but lived by faith and demonstrated God's righteousness.

Ironically, Christ's redemption from the curse of the law is possible by becoming a curse for his followers. "To become a curse" means Jesus did not spare his life, but used his life—and death—to free them from the present evil age (Gal 1:4).[6] In other words, he was faithful to God, discerning the law and fulfilling it until he died. Through his faith, he not only overcame the law's control or condemnation of him but made it complete by loving them. The result is their redemption from the curse of the law because they also may share his faithfulness. So in Christ there is no room for the law to control or condemn them (cf. Rom 8:1). Understood this way, Christ's redemption means they may live in Christ with freedom; they are not under the law or sin because they live by faith.

Christ's redemption of believers "from the curse of the law" in Gal 3:13 can be also understood with an intertext with Rom 7:4–5 and 8:3–4. Paul

6. "The present evil age" is often understood in view of apocalyptic Judaism that God will deliver his people from evil in the future kingdom of God. Paul certainly thinks that way, but the difference is his emphasis on the present status of evil. While salvation will be completed in the parousia, the new life in Christ has already begun. About apocalyptic Judaism, see Byrne, *Galatians and Romans*, 89.

says to the Roman Christians: "You have died to the law through the body of Christ, so that you may belong to another, to him who has been raised from the dead, in order that we may bear fruit for God. While we were living in the flesh, our sinful passions, aroused by the law, were at work in our members to bear fruit for death" (Rom 7:4–5). Here, the law's problem or curse has to do with human sinful passions, which are aroused by the law. In other words, the law is taken by sin and weakened by the flesh, as Rom 8:3 says: "For God has done what the law, weakened by the flesh, could not do: by sending his own Son in the likeness of sinful flesh, and to deal with sin, he condemned sin in the flesh." The real enemy is sin, which seizes an opportunity in the commandment to produce "all kinds of covetousness" (Rom 7:8). In itself, the law is not sin but holy (Rom 7:7–13). Christ was not defeated by sin; rather, he died to sin, which means he was not ruled by it, but he lived by faith for God's righteousness. Sin was condemned because Jesus was not defeated by it, and his faithful work of God fulfilled the law, "so that the just requirement of the law might be fulfilled in us, who walk not according to the flesh but according to the Spirit" (Rom 8:4).

Christ's redemption has a purpose, which is stated in 3:14: "in order that in Christ Jesus the blessing of Abraham might come to the gentiles, so that we might receive the promise of the Spirit through faith." Here "in Christ Jesus" is a modal dative that implies the way of Christ or his faithful dedication to God's righteousness. When people understand and follow the way of Christ, the blessing of Abraham, which is to become his descendants through faith, may come to them. The promise of the Spirit is the same as what God promised Abraham, which is to multiply his descendants. In other words, *anyone* can become a child of God through faith.

In Gal 3:15–16, Paul talks about the importance of promise: "Brothers and sisters, I give an example from daily life: once a person's will has been ratified, no one adds to it or annuls it. Now the promises were made to Abraham and to his offspring; it does not say, 'And to offsprings,' as of many; but it says, 'And to your offspring,' that is, to one person, who is Christ." On the one hand, it is striking that Paul claims that the promises made to Abraham were made to Christ alone, not to many of Abraham's descendants. He seems to devalue Abraham's covenant in the Genesis story where multitudes of his descendants are also promised and blessed. On the other hand, his point is not to reject Abraham's covenant as such, but to point out that Jesus is the Jewish Messiah in whom the original faith story of Abraham culminates. That is, Abraham's blessing is channeled through the radical example of Christ's faith to all who believe. That is why Paul said earlier in 3:14: "in order that in Christ Jesus the blessing of Abraham might come to the gentiles, so that we might receive the promise of the Spirit through faith."

> **Consider and discuss:** Paul talks about Abraham's faith in Galatians. From this, he also talks about Christ's faith(fulness). Why then do many readers and scholars not see the faith(fulness) of Jesus while we see Abraham's faith(fulness)?

D 3:17–18 THE GOSPEL ROOTED IN GOD'S PROMISE

> 17 My point is this: the law, which came four hundred thirty years later, does not annul a covenant previously ratified by God, so as to nullify the promise. 18 For if the inheritance comes from the law, it no longer comes from the promise; but God granted it to Abraham through the promise.

D 3:17–18 is a central unit in the chiasm. Paul reviews what he said in 3:1–16 and concludes it here. His point is the gospel is rooted in God's promise, which cannot be superceded by anything. God's promise is none other than the fact that those who believe like Abraham would be blessed like him. They become descendants of Abraham, that is, children of God. The law cannot cancel God's promise because it is the beginning of the good news. God's promise to Abraham is a spoken word and it should be preferred to anything else. This word of promise is simple and clear. The law was added to the Israelites and came through Moses. It is complex and needs careful interpretation. The law's basic function is regulatory. But the promise of God is affirmative and promises a blessed future to those who live by faith. While the law is holy and good, it does not make persons become Abraham's descendants. What comes first is the promise of God or the Spirit. What makes people descendants of Abraham is the faith that trusts God's promise.

> **Consider and discuss:** Paul traces the root of the gospel to God's promise to Abraham. His point is that God started the good news and decided to include gentiles through faith. If this is the root of the gospel, what is the role/work of Jesus, Son of God?

C' 3:19–21 GOD'S PROMISES DO NOT DEPEND ON THE LAW

19 Why then the law? It was added because of transgressions, until the offspring would come to whom the promise had been made; and it was ordained through angels by a mediator. 20 Now a mediator involves more than one party; but God is one. 21 Is the law then opposed to the promises of God? Certainly not! For if a law had been given that could make alive, then righteousness would indeed come through the law.

Then, *C'* 3:19–21, "God's promises do not depend on the law," clarifies *C* 3:13–16, "Receiving the promise of the Spirit through Christ." That is, God's promise comes through the Spirit and it is fulfilled through Christ. The law was added to check transgressions. Its main function was to guide and discipline the Jewish communities. So the law is necessary and helpful to the community. But it does not replace faith or God's promises that all people will be blessed through Abraham and his faith. Then, Paul says in Gal 3:19b that the law was added "until the offspring would come to whom the promise had been made; and it was ordained through angels by a mediator." It was added until Jesus came; in other words, the law was fulfilled with Christ's coming. Otherwise, Paul does not say the law ended with Christ or that it is useless because of Christ. He does not reject the law, and the point is that the law cannot replace God's promises. Of course, as he says, the law is not against God's promises. The problem is people's dependence on the law without seeing God's promises that all can be his children through faith. What comes first is not the law or even faith, but the promises of God. When one trusts God's promises and lives by faith, one is justified. In this sense, righteousness does not come through the law.

Paul's View of the Law

Paul as a diaspora Jew knows both Jewish tradition and Hellenistic culture. In Jewish scriptures "law" (*torah*) means a few things: 1) the first five books of Moses (the Law or Torah); 2) "teaching" as in Ps 1:2 ("but their delight is in the torah of the Lord, and on his torah they meditate day and night"); 3) particular rules or ordinances that Jews have to keep. In Hellenistic culture, there are two primary concepts of "law" (*nomos*): law as imperial regulations

---

and law as the principle (like "the law of love").[7] Paul uses the law diversely: Jewish law, essence or principle, and law in general. He does not reject the Torah. The only problem is when people stick to the observance of the law without seeing the importance of faith and Jesus's work. Circumcision or food laws may be important to Jews, but they are not the condition for gentiles to join the children of God or to stay in a covenantal community. In Paul's thinking, what comes first is God's promise (grace) and Abraham's faith. While the law is holy and good, it does not come before faith. What Paul opposes is not the law per se but people's insistence on "the works of the law" (such as circumcision and food laws) *as a requirement for gentiles*. As Roetzel says, the problem is "not bad Torah that brings sin and death, . . . but rather the crooked human heart."[8] In other instances, Paul uses the "law" in the sense of "principle": "the law of God" (Rom 7:22, 25; 8:7); "the law of sin" (Rom 7:23, 25; 8:2); "the law of Christ" (Gal 6:2).

B' 3:22–25 THE GOSPEL THROUGH JESUS CHRIST'S FAITHFULNESS

22 But the scripture has imprisoned all things under sin, so that what was promised through *the faithfulness of Jesus Christ* might be given to those who believe. 23 Now before faith came, we were imprisoned and guarded under the law until faith would be revealed. 24 Therefore the law was our guardian until Christ came, so that we might be set right with God by faith. 25 But now that faith has come, we are no longer under a guardian. (Author translation)

B' 3:22–25 corresponds to *B* 3:6–12, "The gospel through Abraham's faith." In *B*, Paul argued that one's justification comes through faith, not by doing the works of the law. There he talked about Abraham's faith and said that those who believe like Abraham would be set right with God. He said that "those who believe are the descendants of Abraham" (Gal 3:7). He also said that the scripture declared the gospel beforehand to Abraham and foresaw that God would justify the gentiles by faith (Gal 3:8). The gospel declared beforehand to Abraham and God's justification of the gentiles by

---

7. In classical Greek, *nomos* often means what we would call "culture" or "custom."

8. Roetzel, *The Letters of Paul*, 116.

faith are realized with the coming of Christ, here in Gal 3:22. That is, the blessing of Abraham comes through Jesus Christ's faithfulness; finally, it is given to those who believe (Gal 3:22; Rom 3:22). Otherwise, the blessing of Abraham does not come to them merely by faith in Christ. First, they must realize the work and faith of Jesus Christ, and then they have to believe and participate in Christ. Here, "those who believe" refers to those who trust God and share Christ's faithfulness.

Until the time of Jesus, Paul says that "the scripture has imprisoned all things under sin" (Gal 3:22), and this statement sounds odd because the scripture is seen negatively. His use of the scripture seems inconsistent, when compared with Gal 3:8 in which the scripture is presented in a good light, as it declared the gospel beforehand to Abraham and foresaw God's work of justification of the gentiles by faith. But now, he talks about the seemingly negative view of the scripture that imprisoned all things under the power of sin. His point is this: with the coming of Jesus and through his faithfulness, the blessing promised to the gentiles came to be realized. With Christ's faithful work and sacrifice, sin also loses power because he died to it. Before Christ came, sin has been in control of all things and humans. But now is different because of Jesus Christ.

In Gal 3:23–25, Paul continues to emphasize Christ's fulfillment of the law. As we saw before in Gal 3:6–21, here the fulfillment language is not to be understood as Christ's replacing of the law or faith's overthrowing of it (cf. Rom 3:31). Therefore, Gal 3:23 needs careful attention: "Now before faith came, we were imprisoned and guarded under the law until faith would be revealed." Here "faith" refers to trust in God and belief in the promises of God or the Spirit. Faith, actually, has been working even before Jesus. Abraham had faith in God and many of God's agents were faithful. Therefore, Paul seems to contradict himself since faith did *not* begin with Jesus. Nevertheless, he concludes that Jesus is the Jewish Messiah who made a radical shift about faith, and his faithfulness is the basis and moment of a new time and a new life in the Spirit. In this sense, "faith" in Gal 3:23 is Jesus's faithfulness, which is the basis of the Christian life. He interprets the law with a focus on Christ Jesus and thinks that until this radical time of Christ's faithfulness, Jews were imprisoned and guarded *under the law* (*hypo nomon*), which includes both the Jewish law and other laws including Roman laws under which people had to live. In other words, Paul points out the time sin and the law ruled before Christ Jesus came.

However, Paul's point is not that the law is temporary, outdated, or useless after Christ came. For him, the law is holy and good (cf. Rom 7:12). His metaphor *paidagōgos* (guardian) relating to the law does not point to the law's failure. In Roman society, *paidagōgos* could have a "positive" meaning as well as a "negative" meaning. The positive meaning has to do with a guardian who is responsible for taking a child to school and bringing him back home. A guardian's role is important in helping minors to grow safely, protecting them from potential dangers on the streets. For example, we see the positive image of a guardian in 1 Cor 4:15: "For though you might have ten thousand guardians in Christ, you do not have many fathers. Indeed, in Christ Jesus I became your father through the gospel." Here "guardians" are teachers who are necessary to people. Even though Paul says he is a father to the Corinthians to emphasize his personal relationship with them, he does not negate the role of guardians, who are teachers of Christ.[9]

Then, what is the law's relation to Christ? The answer is the law was fulfilled in Christ who gave himself to free people from the evil age (1:4). Christ's fulfillment of the law does not require us to reject the law or its validity. God gave the law to Jews not to convict them but to help them to live a life of freedom, justice, and peace. But it did not work well. So God sent his Son to fulfill the law's requirement, which is to do justice and love mercy (Mic 6:8). This idea is also seen in Rom 8:1-4:

> 1 There is therefore now no condemnation for those who are in Christ Jesus. 2 For the law of the Spirit of life in Christ Jesus has set you free from the law of sin and of death. 3 For God has done what the law, weakened by the flesh, could not do: by sending his own Son in the likeness of sinful flesh, and to deal with sin, he condemned sin in the flesh, 4 so that the just requirement of the law might be fulfilled in us, who walk not according to the flesh but according to the Spirit.

In the above passage, Paul's point is that Jesus defeated the law of sin and of death, which means he was not controlled by sin. Rather, Jesus resisted it, and his resistance brought him to death by the evil powers of the Roman Empire. In fact, if the law had worked well and deterred sin and brought

---

9. Dale B. Martin, Emeritus Professor of Religious Studies at Yale University, supports my point, in an email sent to me: "Paul refuses to use paidagogos for himself, preferring the 'better' role of 'father.' And Paul knows that some of those they would have considered their pedagogues in Christ did *not* treat the Corinthians well. See 2 Cor 10-13, where Paul sarcastically contrasts his 'gentle' treatment of the Corinthians with the 'harsh' treatment they endured from their 'superapostles.'"

justice to people, God would have not sent his Son. But the law was weakened by the flesh, which means the law did not function well because of human sinful passions. But God could do what is impossible by sending his Son in the likeness of sinful flesh, which means Jesus defeated sin through faithfulness. He lived in the sinful world but did not submit to sin. So sin was condemned by God. All those who follow Jesus may have a new life in the Spirit. As we see above, Paul's point is not that the law is itself a problem but that it did not function well because of the flesh or sinful passions. The law is not replaced by Jesus but *fulfilled* by him. Now is the time of faith, which came through Christ, and those who follow Christ will fulfill the law. Logically, what people have to follow is not the law but Christ who fulfilled the law. If they die with Christ and die to sin, they would not be under sin or the law. So Paul says in Gal 3:25: "But now that faith has come, we are no longer under a guardian." In the end, his point is this: The law as a guardian is limited because it is under human control and subject to human interpretation. So the true guardian is Christ who embodied God's promise through faith. Therefore, people have to follow Christ's faithfulness.

A' 3:26–29 A NEW VISION OF THE COMMUNITY IN CHRIST

> 26 for in Christ Jesus you are all children of God through faith. 27 As many of you as were baptized into Christ have clothed yourselves with Christ. 28 There is no longer Jew or Greek, there is no longer slave or free, there is no longer male and female; for all of you are one in Christ Jesus. 29 And if you belong to Christ, then you are Abraham's offspring, heirs according to the promise.

A' 3:26–29 corresponds to A 3:1–5, "Confusion in the church due to the lack of faith" and presents a solution to the issue of confusion, which has to do with Jewish laws such as circumcision and other works of the law. The churches of Galatia are confused about Paul's gospel. He taught that gentiles do not need circumcision, but some people say gentile Christians must be circumcised in addition to faith. So Paul reaffirms his gospel and presents a new vision of the community in Christ. Thus, he says in Gal 3:26: "for in Christ Jesus you are all children of God through faith." Now all people—regardless of their ethnicity, social status, or gender—can be heirs of God through faith. This is possible when they are in Christ, which means when they follow the example of Christ's faithfulness. "In Christ" is a modal dative that implies the way of Christ, the life he lived by faith to reveal who God is. Two things are needed to become children of God, in addition to the grace or promise of God: these are indicated by the phrases "in Christ" and "through faith." The former implies that the followers of Jesus have to base their faith in Christ. The latter means they have to live by faith, not through the law or any culture. With this in mind, the proper translation of Gal 3:26 should not be the NIV's: "You are all sons of God through faith in Christ Jesus." This translation looks like it supports the doctrine of "justification by faith" in that what is needed is believers' faith in Christ. But here Paul's emphasis is not to make Christ the object of faith. Rather, his point is to make Christians follow Christ's faithfulness. That is how we read "in Christ" and "through faith" separately. So the NRSV makes better sense: "for in Christ Jesus you are all children of God through faith."

Then, in Gal 3:27, Paul reminds them of their previous status that they were baptized into Christ and have clothed themselves with Christ. In Gal 3:26, the tense is the present, which indicates the ideal status in that all can be children of God through faith. But in Gal 3:27, the tense is the past aorist, which refers to the previous times when Paul proclaimed the gospel to them. At that time, they accepted the gospel through faith and followed Jesus. They received the promise of the Spirit. In other words, they were baptized into Christ, which means they have died with Christ. It also means they have clothed themselves with Christ. In other words, they are to live like Christ, as a garment represents a person's identity and work.

In Gal 3:28, Paul goes back to the ideal status of a community in Christ: "There is no longer Jew or Greek, there is no longer slave or free, there is no longer male and female; for all of you are one in Christ Jesus." This verse should not be read as a future eschatological event when all differences and distinctions may disappear, when we will be like the angels.[10] But in the immediate context of the Galatians who are confused about Paul's gospel, what they need is not the future status of salvation as such, but livable, reliable community of love and care in Christ. They need a clear vision of a new life in Christ. However, Paul's vision of a community in Christ is not a radical egalitarian community that erases all differences or distinctions in terms of ethnicity, social class, and gender. While maintaining their social status or ethnic and gender differences, all people regardless of their status can join a Christian community freely through faith. Once they gather, they

10. In this eschatological view, "no longer male and female" points to a sexless status like that of an angel.

have to love one another and respect each other. In the community, they are free to participate in worship. They are all given equal care and support.[11]

As we see above, Paul's language of "one in Christ Jesus" is not about radical equality in Christ or in society. Rather, his point is that now the gospel was proclaimed and that *any person*—regardless of his or her ethnicity, class, or gender—can come to God through faith. Otherwise, he does not aim to abolish evil laws or systems such as slavery or the oppression of human beings by the Roman Empire. This is because he thinks, eventually, all human systems and differences would disappear on the day of the parousia when God will intervene in the world.

But it does not mean that Paul has no interest in the transformation of a person, community, or society. Indeed, he never tells the churches that they can only wait for the Lord without working hard. Rather, his advice is to show good works of God in the world so that people may come to God. Also, he exhorts them to engage in the world with love and care for other people. For example, in Rom 12:2, he asks the Roman Christians to be transformed: "Do not be conformed to this world, but be transformed by the renewing of your minds, so that you may discern what is the will of God—what is good and acceptable and perfect."

In the end, Gal 3:28 is not a de facto statement about the radical status of human liberation and equality in the sense that there is no longer any distinction between free and slave, Jew and Greek, male and female. Rather, Paul's point is that now, because of Christ, all people, regardless of their ethnicity, social class, or gender, can be children of God without differences. Otherwise, he does not talk about the eradication of gender, ethnicity, or social class. That is because of his view of eschatology, that the Lord would come back soon to correct all maladies and injustices.

Having said this, perhaps the image of a hot tub (whirlpool) in a fitness center may be a helpful analogy to Paul's description of a community in Gal 3:28. Members of a fitness center, regardless of who they are in terms of ethnicity, class, and gender, can enter the common hot tub and enjoy it. In the tub, there are all kinds of people, young and old, men and women, and rich and poor. But they enjoy the pool in the same place. Like this

---

11. In Paul's church, men and women equally receive the gift of the Spirit and freely participate in worship and work together for the gospel (1 Cor 12–14). In 1 Cor 11, women actively participate in worship. Phoebe is an apostle in the Roman house church (Rom 16:7). But as time goes by, in post-Pauline churches women are checked and prevented from teaching (for example 1 Tim 2:11–15).

image of a pool, in Paul's church, any person can join through faith and enjoy a new life in the Spirit.

In sum, "all of you are one in Christ Jesus" (Gal 3:28) means that the Galatians, wherever they came from, must be united with one another through faith working through love (Gal 5:14). They have to respect and love one another. Here "one" connotes the status of the union, not the unity made up of hierarchy, as in Stoicism, or an eschatological status like angels, or the radical revolutionary status, as in a radical human liberation project. Rather, Paul's point is anyone can belong to Christ through faith, and then he or she is Abraham's offspring, "heirs according to the promise" (Gal 3:29). Formerly, Jews thought they were the only children of God, but God's covenantal love extends to all people.

> **Consider and discuss:** As we saw above, Paul's politics is a bit am-
> biguous since he is not a social reformer or revolutionary. He does
> not promote slavery either, as opposed to the household codes in
> the Deutero-Pauline and Pastoral Letters. This seemingly luke-
> warm position is apparently due to the interim ethics that teach
> that God will eventually fix the human world on the day of the
> parousia. With the above in mind, how do you interpret Gal 3:28?

SECTION V

4:1–31

The Advantage of the Gospel

AFTER BASING HIS GOSPEL in the promise of God (Gal 3:1–29), in Gal 4:1–31, Paul moves on to talk about the advantage of the gospel. He reminds the Galatians that God sent his Son to deliver them from slavery and that he has sent the spirit of his Son into their hearts because they are his children. All this means God cares for them. But in reality, this advantage of the gospel is in danger because they are turning back to the elemental spirits, "observing special days, and months, and seasons, and years" (Gal 4:10). Therefore, Paul asks them to return to the gospel that he proclaimed, so that they may stand in the truth of the gospel (Gal 4:12–20). Finally, Paul speaks to the law-adherents in the church and makes sure they understand that the blessing of the children of God does not come through the law but through the promise. Then he uses an allegory of Sarah and Hagar to make the case. With all these divisions above, we also see a chiasm of *ABB'A'* in this section, Gal 4:1–31. See below.

> *A* 4:1–7 God's assurance of his children
> > *B* 4:8–11 How can you turn back again to the elemental spirits?
> > *B'* 4:12–20 Return to the gospel
> *A'* 4:21–31 "We are children, not of the slave but of the free woman"

A 4:1–7 GOD'S ASSURANCE OF HIS CHILDREN

1 My point is this: heirs, as long as they are minors, are no better than slaves, though they are the owners of all the property; 2 but they remain under guardians and trustees until the date set by the father. 3 So with us; while we were minors, we were enslaved to the elemental spirits of the world. 4 But when the fullness of time had come, God sent his Son, born of a woman, born under the law, 5 in order to redeem those who were under the law, so that we might receive adoption as children. 6 And because you are children, God has sent the spirit of his Son into our hearts, crying, "Abba! Father!" 7 So you are no longer a slave but a child, and if a child then also an heir, through God.

In A 4:1–7, "God's assurance of his children," Paul reminds the Galatians that they became children of God through the grace of God. He also reminds them they were previously enslaved to the power of the world, using an example of inheritance law in society (Gal 4:1–3). Heirs are entitled to receive an inheritance. But if they are minors, they cannot receive it. In that sense, they are no better than slaves who are not entitled. So heirs remain under guardians and trustees until a later day set by the father. This analogy applies to the Galatians, who were enslaved to the elemental spirits of the world (Gal 4:3). (The expression "elemental spirits of the world" is vague. Perhaps Paul means that they worshiped foreign gods and various spirits in the world.) Their status as "minors" implies that *as heirs* they could not yet take control of the inheritance. But Jews were also "minors" if they were not mature heirs.

Then in Gal 4:4, Paul shifts his tone and says: "But when the fullness of time had come, God sent his Son, born of a woman, born under the law." "The fullness of time" falls under God's providence, and Paul does not clearly explain what he means by the expression. God's sending of his Son in the right time is a theological statement meaning that Jesus worked for God and on behalf of people. Otherwise, the language of "sending of his Son" is not to be taken literally in the sense that he came down from heaven. In Jewish thinking and in the Old Testament, the concept of son of God applies to individual persons or to Israel, and it is not a divine title. Adam is the son of God in the sense that he resembles God's image, and in fact, in Luke 3:38, he is called "son of God." King David is also called the son of God. At other times, Israel as a whole is called God's son (Exod 4:22–23; Hos 11:1). A particular individual is also called the son of God

(Isa 7:14). The son of God title is also used by the emperor Augustus, who is called *divi filius*, which means "son of a god." Given the above context, speaking of Jesus as the Son of God would have been acceptable. But for Paul, Jesus is a unique son of God, who fulfills the law and sets people free from the evil age (Gal 1:4).

At the same time, Paul thinks of Jesus as a human being "born of a woman," which implies his birth is ordinary just like any other human being. Paul never talks about Jesus's virgin birth. He probably knew that Jesus was born just like any other human being. Then, he also says Jesus was born "under the law," implying both the human convention of the laws and Jewish law.[1] Jesus had to deal with Roman laws, especially the imperial control of the Jewish land. He grew up in Nazareth and saw corruption and the exploitation of everyday people. The people of his village suffered from poverty and many of them became landless. He also had to live under the Jewish law, but his interpretation of the law was different from others. He was like a Pharisee in terms of his passion for the scripture and reforming society. But he was not a strict observer like Pharisees. In other words, the law was not at the center of his religiosity. Rather, he reinterpreted the law carefully and practiced the love of God radically, sitting and eating with sinners. The law to him was a means of loving God and neighbor.

> **Consider and discuss:** "Born of a woman" may have various meanings.
>
> Do you think the phrase "born of a woman" may signify Jesus's "human birth," rather than a miraculous birth as in Matthew's birth narrative? Paul never mentions such a miraculous birth in his letters. When he mentions Jesus's humanity in Rom 1:3–4, he emphasizes only Jesus's lineage to David: "the gospel concerning his Son, who was descended from David according to the flesh and was declared to be Son of God with power according to the spirit of holiness by resurrection from the dead, Jesus Christ our Lord." Paul contrasts Jesus's humanity with his resurrection. If Paul emphasizes Jesus's humanity in context with this phrase "born of a woman," why does he do so? Why do you think Paul uses the expression "born of a woman"?

In Gal 4:5, Jesus being born of a woman and under the law was to redeem those who were under the law. Here, "those who were under the law"

---

1. There is no definite article in *hypo nomon (under law)* so the phrase may be inclusive of various sense of the law.

means all who live under the law in the sense of bondage or slavery. While the Jewish law is holy, it may become a means of control of others. While Roman laws may be good in some aspects, they may serve the powerful and elites. While Jesus was born in the world as a vulnerable human being and experienced all sorts of injustices ("born of a woman and born under the law"), he was not controlled by the law, whether the Jewish law or Roman laws. He did not become a slave of the law, but he did the work of God and fulfilled the law. His work of God is to liberate those who are "under the law," which means those who are controlled by the Jewish law or Roman laws. Here "under the law," as noted before, implies two circumstances: the human convention of the laws and the Jewish law. Once they are freed from slavery to the law or from the power of sin, they become children of God (Gal 4:5).[2]

In Gal 4:6, Paul emphasizes that God's children are taken care of by the Spirit: "And because you are children, God has sent the spirit of his Son into our hearts, crying, 'Abba! Father!'" God's sending of the spirit of his Son is a new idea that we have not seen in this letter, though it appears in his other letters: Rom 8:9 and Phil 1:19. Jesus was exalted by God and is in heaven now, but God sent the spirit of his Son to his children. This implies that God cares for them and sends the Spirit of Jesus to help them in their new life in the Spirit.[3] It also implies that Jesus cares for God's children and obeys him. The Spirit of Jesus cries, "Abba! Father!" This crying refers to Jesus crying at many moments during his public ministry. For example, he taught his disciples to pray to God the Father, who is in heaven (Matt 6:9–13; Luke 11:2–4). He prayed at Gethsemane, calling God "Abba, Father": "Abba, Father, for you all things are possible; remove this cup from

2. Becoming children of God is a great advantage to the Galatians. But in order to live as children of God, they need participation in Christ. We already saw this in Gal 3:22: "so that what was promised through the faith of Jesus might be given to those who believe." Here "through the faith of Jesus" indicates that God's blessing and promises given to Abraham came through Jesus's faithfulness. Now the followers of Jesus need the same faith of Jesus to enjoy that same blessing. Likewise, Paul says in Gal 3:26: "for in Christ Jesus you are all children of God through faith." Here "in Christ Jesus" as a modal dative requires the Galatians to live like Christ Jesus and imitate his faithfulness. Their faithful living in Christ is expressed "through faith" (*dia tēs pisteōs*). Interestingly, there is a definite article *tēs* before *pisteōs*, which implies this faith is Jesus's. Namely, they become children of God through the faith that Jesus had, which is none other than Christians' participation in Christ.

3. "For you did not receive a spirit of slavery to fall back into fear, but you have received a spirit of adoption. When we cry, 'Abba! Father!' it is that very Spirit bearing witness with our spirit that we are children of God" (Rom 8.15).

me; yet, not what I want, but what you want" (Mark 14:36). In a desperate moment like this, Jesus sought God's will and he followed it.

Then in Gal 4:7, Paul says: "So you are no longer a slave but a child, and if a child then also an heir, through God." "A child" means now the Galatians have to live as children of God, which means they must follow the way of Christ and live a life of freedom with his Spirit. They should not be chained in slavery to the law or any restraints of the laws, including Roman laws. Eventually, God is the one who called Abraham and sent his Son to redeem those who are in slavery to sin. Jesus served God and was faithful to him. What one becomes is not a child of Jesus but a child of God. That is why "through God" (Gal 4:7) is important to becoming children of God.

Consider and discuss: Interestingly, Paul talks about the Spirit of Jesus, who will be sent by God to assure his followers about their place in God (Gal 4:6). Why do you think Paul talks about the Spirit of *Jesus* instead of "the Spirit of God"? Similarly, in 1 Cor 15:45, he also presents Jesus as "a life-giving spirit": "The first man, Adam, became a living being; the last Adam became a life-giving spirit." Do you see any common ground between Gal 4:6 and 1 Cor 15:45? What does "a life-giving spirit" mean and why does Paul talk about this in the Corinthian context?

B 4:8–11 HOW CAN YOU TURN BACK AGAIN TO THE ELEMENTAL SPIRITS?

8 Formerly, when you did not know God, you were enslaved to beings that by nature are not gods. 9 Now, however, that you have come to know God, or rather to be known by God, how can you turn back again to the weak and beggarly elemental spirits? How can you want to be enslaved to them again? 10 You are observing special days, and months, and seasons, and years. 11 I am afraid that my work for you may have been wasted.

In Gal 4:8–11, Paul contrasts the Galatians' former life with their current status. Before they knew God, they were worshippers of gods. But now they have come to know God through Paul's proclamation of the good news of God. Paul reminds them of their new life in Christ, received when he proclaimed the gospel to them. They accepted God's love and Jesus's grace and decided to live by the Spirit through faith (cf. Gal 1:6). But now the advantage of the gospel is in danger because they are turning back again to their former pagan lifestyle, worshipping non-gods, being enslaved to "elemental spirits" (Gal 4:9), which refer to all beliefs and practices involving in the worship of other gods. So he asks: "How can you want to be enslaved to them again?" (Gal 4:9). They are now "observing special days, and months, and seasons, and years" (Gal 4:10). In other words, they participate in various forms of pagan lifestyle, believing astrology, accepting mysticism or mystery religions. So Paul worries that his work may have been wasted (Gal 4:11).

The fundamental problem in the churches of Galatia is about the confusion of the gospel whose center is Christ's faithfulness. The danger in the community occurs when the Galatians move away from this faith-focused work and resort either to the law or return to paganism.

B' 4:12–20 RETURN TO THE GOSPEL

12 Friends, I beg you, become as I am, for I also have become as you are. You have done me no wrong. 13 You know that it was because of a physical infirmity that I first announced the gospel to you; 14 though my condition put you to the test, you did not scorn or despise me, but welcomed me as an angel of God, as Christ Jesus. 15 What has become of the goodwill you felt? For I testify that, had it been possible, you would have torn out your eyes and given them to me. 16 Have I now become your enemy by telling you the truth? 17 They make much of you, but for no good purpose; they want to exclude you, so that you may make much of them. 18 It is good to be made much of for a good purpose at all times, and not only when I am present with you. 19 My little children, for whom I am again in the pain of childbirth until Christ is formed in you, 20 I wish I were present with you now and could change my tone, for I am perplexed about you.

In *B'* 4:12–20, Paul asks the Galatians to return to the gospel that he proclaimed to them. In doing so, he asks them to become like him as he became like them (Gal 4:12). In other words, he begs them to remember the time of his gospel proclamation when he was suffering from a physical ailment, the specifics of which he does not mention (Gal 4:13). He also understood their miserable situation and loved them. As an evangelist, he was expected to show that he was strong. But he was not strong enough to show them his abilities in speech or physical health. They understood his situation and welcomed him without scoring or despising him (Gal 4:14). They welcomed him as an angel of God, as Christ Jesus. Paul remembers such a time of joy that they not only accepted his gospel but welcomed him in spite of his physical illness. They treated him as best they possibly could, as they would an angel of God. There was such a strong emotional, spiritual intimacy and understanding between them.

Then, to his dismay, they forgot all of the good things they received from God. So he asks: "Where then is the great attitude that you had? I swear that, if possible, you would have dug out your eyes and given them to me" (Gal 4:15, CEB). Even though he was surprised by their sudden change of mind, he still reminds them of such a good time to which they need to return. But before that, they must understand correctly what he proclaimed. So he asks: "Have I now become your enemy by telling you the truth?" (4:16). Here the truth is about the gospel he proclaimed to them; namely, the gospel is for all through faith. For him, the truth of the gospel is well expressed in Rom 1:16: "For I am not ashamed of the gospel; it is the power of God for salvation to everyone who has faith, to the Jew first and also to the Greek" (Rom 1:16). He challenged those who depend on the law or the works of the law to the detriment of faith because they are not really concerned with the wellbeing of the gentile Christians. Rather, they use them for their power, as he says: "They are so concerned about you, though not with good intentions. Rather, they want to shut you out so that you would run after them" (Gal 4:17, CEB).

> **Consider and discuss:** Paul talks about "the truth of the gospel" in Gal 2:5 and 2:14. And he also says similarly in Gal 4:16: "Have I now become your enemy by telling you the truth?" What is the truth of the gospel Paul is eager to share and defend? Why does he say he became their enemy by telling the truth? Is this the same as "the truth of the gospel" he mentioned earlier?

Then, in Gal 4:18–21, he expresses his desire to return to them and to help them right away. It is important to have good people with good intentions (Gal 4:18). Good people means those who live according to the truth of the gospel and help others to grow in faith. Paul calls the Galatians "little children" and wants to nourish them again as if he were a mother going through labor pains (Gal 4:19). The goal of his labor pains is not to produce little Pauls but to form Christ in them. In other words, his job is to help them accept the grace of Christ, so that they may live for God through faith.

The image here echoes Paul's confession about Christ in Gal 2:20: "and it is no longer I who live, but it is Christ who lives in me. And the life I now live in the flesh I live *by the faith of the Son of God*, who loved me and gave himself for me." He wants to do this job of re-nourishing them right away, so he wishes to be present with them (Gal 4:20).

A 4:21–31 "WE ARE CHILDREN, NOT OF THE SLAVE BUT OF THE FREE WOMAN"

21 Tell me, you who desire to be subject to the law, will you not listen to the law? 22 For it is written that Abraham had two sons, one by a slave woman and the other by a free woman. 23 One, the child of the slave, was born according to the flesh; the other, the child of the free woman, was born through the promise. 24 Now this is an allegory: these women are two covenants. One woman, in fact, is Hagar, from Mount Sinai, bearing children for slavery. 25 Now Hagar is Mount Sinai in Arabia and corresponds to the present Jerusalem, for she is in slavery with her children. 26 But the other woman corresponds to the Jerusalem above; she is free, and she is our mother. 27 For it is written, "Rejoice, you childless one, you who bear no children, burst into song and shout, you who endure no birth pangs; for the children of the desolate woman are more numerous than the children of the one who is married." 28 Now you, my friends, are children of the promise, like Isaac. 29 But just as at that time the child who was born according to the flesh persecuted the child who was born according to the Spirit, so it is now also. 30 But what does the scripture say? "Drive out the slave and her child; for the child of the slave will not share the inheritance with the child of the free woman." 31 So then, friends, we are children, not of the slave but of the free woman.

In 4:21–31, Paul strengthens his point made in 4:1–7, which is God's assurance of his children. He begins with the following: "Tell me, those of you who want to be *under law (hypo nomon)*, will you not listen to *the law (ton nomon)*." The former ("under law") without a definite article, as we saw in Gal 4:5, means more than the Jewish scripture or the works of the law; it also means human conventions of laws including Roman laws. But the latter ("listen to *the* law") with a definite article, might mean the Jewish scripture in general, which is a positive sense, as he asks: "Will you not listen to the law (scripture)?"

Then he talks about the story of Sarah and Hagar in the scripture, saying: "For it is written that Abraham had two sons, one by a slave woman and the other by a free woman. One, the child of the slave, was born according to the flesh; the other, the child of the free woman, was born through the promise" (Gal 4:22–23). In fact, this story is a difficult one to digest. From a critical narrative perspective, this story reveals Sarah's anxiety, dislike, and mercilessness toward Hagar and her son Ishmael. It also shows Abraham's unfair behavior toward them. He agrees to Sarah's request that they be expelled. Of course, God tells him to do so (Gen 21:12–13). But this story is told from the narrator's perspective in that God allows him to do this to secure the inheritance for Isaac. What we see in the story is Sarah's preemptive strike on Hagar and Ishmael. But from a critical narrative perspective, the story presents itself a very ethical problem about God. How would a good God allow Abraham to cast them out? Do we see a good part of the story here while we witness innocent persons being expelled for no good reason? A more palatable part of the story comes when God takes care of Hagar and Ishmael in the desert, promising another great nation. Though if God really takes care of them, we might feel that he should not have allowed them to be expelled in the first place. God in this story reflects the theology or ideology of the narrator of this story.

Having said this, now we can look into Paul's allegorical interpretation of this story. In Gal 4:24a, he says: "These things are an allegory: the women are two covenants." He focuses not on Abraham or Isaac or Ishmael but on the two women, Hagar and Sarah. The former is from Mount Sinai in Arabia and bears children for slavery (Gal 4:24). This logic is based on the story in Gen 21 where Hagar is not chosen by God and expelled by Abraham. But Paul twists this story and says now Hagar corresponds to the present Jerusalem (Gal 4:25), which is a metaphor pointing to a status or situation that God is not present with people. In other words, when people do not depend on the promise of God or rest on faith, they are not children of God. But the other woman, Sarah, "corresponds to the Jerusalem above; she is free, and she is our mother" (Gal 4:26). "The Jerusalem above" is also a metaphor pointing to the reverse counterpart of the present Jerusalem. The Jerusalem above does not have to be understood as a "heavenly Jerusalem" that connotes a future eschatological place. Rather, it points to a status or situation in which God is present with people. When they depend on the promise of God and rely on faith they can live as his children. In the allegory, Sarah looked to God and trusted his promise about a child. She is not bound by any human conventions of the law or any laws. She just believes the promise of God. So she is free because nothing could prevent her from believing it. In the end, Paul says, "she is our mother," which means all who have faith are her children, the children of freedom who depend on the promise of God. In Gal 4:27, Paul quotes from Isa 54:1 and confirms the blessing of Sarah: "Rejoice, you childless one, you who bear no children, burst into song and shout, you who endure no birth pangs; for the children of the desolate woman are more numerous than the children of the one who is married."[4]

In Gal 4:28, Paul addresses the Galatians: "Now you, my brothers and sisters, are children of the promise, like Isaac." He calls them brothers (*adelphoi*), including both men and women, and tells them they are children (*tekna*) of the promise, like Isaac. Because they believe in the promise of God, they are the children of God. Their priority is faith in God through Christ, and it is not in the law or the works of the law.

In Gal 4:29, Paul reminds them that there may be difficulties or persecution due to their faith: "But just as at that time the child who was born according to the flesh persecuted the child who was born according to the Spirit, so it is now also." In this situation, his advice is they get distance from a different gospel proclaimed by others, saying: "But what does the scripture say? 'Drive out the slave and her child; for the child of the slave will not share the inheritance with the child of the free woman'" (Gal 4:30). They cannot compromise the truth of the gospel he proclaimed to them. Finally, in Gal 4:31, he reiterates his point: "So then, brothers and sisters, we are children, not of the slave but of the free woman."

Consider and discuss: Paul uses an allegory of Sarah and Hagar to get his point across. But in doing so, he makes Hagar once again marginalized and miserable. In the Genesis story (Gen 21), Hagar is a victim of Sarah, Abraham, and God. Eventually, God blesses her and her son Ishmael. Paul's allegory of Sarah and Hagar may work for Paul, but it is not ethically sound. Similarly, the conquest story of Joshua in the Hebrew Bible may work for Jews as a theological story, though it is not ethically sound. But to the Canaanites, Palestinians, and American Indians, it is a tormenting story that cannot be erased as long as it is told.[5] What do you think

---

4. Regarding Paul's use of maternal imagery, see Eastman, *Recovering Paul's Mother Tongue*, 63–123. She finds the positive image of maternal imagery in Paul's theology and talks about the power of transformation of the gospel.

5. Israelites were oppressed by Egyptians, but God liberated them from slavery in

about Paul's use of allegory in this way? Is there a better way to get his point across?

Egypt. That is an Exodus story of liberation. But as time went, soon they became oppressors/conquerors to the Canaanites because God told them to take the land by destroying everything. Is this a good story? Robert Allen Warrior points out the problem of reading the above narratives as stories of liberation and oppression. He writes as an American Indian and challenges the Jewish reading of the above stories. See Warrior, "Canaanites, Cowboys, and Indians." He says European settlers came to America, seeking freedom from persecution. When they got here, they thought America was given as a promised land and turned oppressors, expelling many of the American Indians.

SECTION VI

5:1—6:10

The Mandate of the Gospel

THUS FAR PAUL HAS taken sufficient time to explain where his gospel came from (Gal 1:11—2:10) and clarified it in relation to Jewish law and culture (Gal 2:11–21). He also rooted the gospel in the very promises of God made to Abraham, which were fulfilled through Jesus (Gal 3:1–29). All those who have the faith of Jesus will receive the same blessing made to Abraham. He also clarified the advantage of the gospel, which is to become children of God (Gal 4:1–31). Because the Galatians are children of God, God takes care of them and sends the spirit of his Son Jesus. Now he moves on to the last section of his gospel before closing: "the mandate of the gospel" (Gal 5:1—6:10), a summary of his gospel that takes the form of exhortation to the Galatian community.[1] In this section, we find several forms of the mandate of the gospel. In Gal 5:1–15, the focus of the mandate is "Stand firm in Christ; Do not submit again to a yoke of slavery." In Gal 5:16–26, the mandate is "Live by the Spirit." Lastly, in Gal 6:1–10, the mandate of the gospel is "Fulfill the law of Christ."

---

1. Some may think Paul moved from the law-free gospel in the first four chapters of Galatians to law-fulfilling in the last two chapters. But this view is incorrect because Paul never claimed that the gospel rejects the law. Rather, there is consistency between the former and the latter in terms of the law and faith. That is, what is wrong is not the law but the lack of faith. Frank Matera also sees the connection between the first four chapters of Galatians and the last two chapters. He says Gal 5–6 fulfills the law. See, Matera, *Galatians*, 196.

5:1–15 "STAND FIRM IN CHRIST; DO NOT SUBMIT AGAIN TO A YOKE OF SLAVERY"

1 For freedom Christ has set us free. Stand firm, therefore, and do not submit again to a yoke of slavery. 2 Listen! I, Paul, am telling you that if you let yourselves be circumcised, Christ will be of no benefit to you. 3 Once again I testify to every man who lets himself be circumcised that he is obliged to obey the entire law. 4 You who want to be justified by the law have cut yourselves off from Christ; you have fallen away from grace. 5 For through the Spirit, by faith, we eagerly wait for the hope of righteousness. 6 For in Christ Jesus neither circumcision nor uncircumcision counts for anything; the only thing that counts is faith working through love. 7 You were running well; who prevented you from obeying the truth? 8 Such persuasion does not come from the one who calls you. 9 A little yeast leavens the whole batch of dough. 10 I am confident about you in the Lord that you will not think otherwise. But whoever it is that is confusing you will pay the penalty. 11 But my friends, why am I still being persecuted if I am still preaching circumcision? In that case the offense of the cross has been removed. 12 I wish those who unsettle you would castrate themselves! 13 For you were called to freedom, brothers and sisters; only do not use your freedom as an opportunity for self-indulgence, but through love become slaves to one another. 14 For the whole law is summed up in a single commandment, "You shall love your neighbor as yourself." 15 If, however, you bite and devour one another, take care that you are not consumed by one another.

In Gal 5:1, Paul states the mandate of the gospel: "Christ has set us free for freedom. Stand firm, therefore, and do not submit again to a yoke of slavery." Earlier in Gal 1:4, he talked about Christ's love and faith. Because of his love and moral sacrifice for people, they may live a new life of freedom in Christ. Paul reminds the Galatians that they are set free from all bondage that shackles them because of Christ and their participation in Christ. No one or nothing can take away their freedom. No circumcision or any works of the law can replace the work of Christ and God's promise. But at the same time, he reminds them that their freedom has a purpose; it is for freedom (*tē eleutheria*), saying "Christ has set us free *for freedom.*" Those who experience freedom in Christ must use their freedom for others, not for self-promotion or individualistic freedom. Gaining freedom is not itself the goal of freedom. In this regard, Paul's view of freedom is different from Stoicism in which freedom is largely understood as inner peace (a status of *apatheia*). It is also different from the enthusiasts or libertines who think they were already saved and are free in Christ and therefore can do anything. For Paul, freedom results from Christ's work and it can be realized when one participates in Christ. It also has the purpose of edifying the community. As Christ worked for others, this freedom must be used for them. So Paul says in 1 Cor 6:12: "'All things are lawful for me,' but not all things are beneficial. 'All things are lawful for me,' but I will not be dominated by anything." He reminds the Corinthians that their freedom is for edifying the community and that it should not be used irresponsibly, such as for sleeping with a prostitute or doing evil. His advice to them is: "For you were bought with a price; therefore glorify God in your body" (1 Cor 6:20). The price here is Christ's giving of his life, so freedom is not free. The Corinthians, therefore, should be careful about their body and be united to Christ, which means to live by his faithfulness. This same thing also applies to the Galatians. They were bought with a price, which is Christ's redemptive work for them (Gal 1:4).

In 5:1b, Paul says "Stand firm." That is, the Galatians should stand firm with Christ who has set them free from the present evil age (1:4). Their standing is not by themselves or for themselves. It is rooted in the way of Christ and his faithfulness to God. In order to stay in freedom, they have to strive to maintain their freedom by following the way of Christ. When they follow Christ and die with him, they may overcome their sinful passions. Therefore, he advises them: "do not submit again to a yoke of slavery" (Gal 5:1c). A "yoke of slavery" refers to anything that prevents them from enjoying or staying in freedom. In the context of the churches of Galatia, it has to do with the way of Jewish laws or culture. So immediately, he says in Gal 5:2, "Listen! I, Paul, am telling you that if you let yourselves be circumcised, Christ will be of no benefit to you." Here, Paul's point is that the Galatians should not depend on the law or works of the law; rather, they must know Christ's work of liberation and accept the promise of God through faith. They must hold fast to the freedom that came through Jesus.

> **Consider and discuss:** In Galatians, freedom does not mean absolute individual freedom as in the sense of Western democratic values that a person is born free and stays free. In Paul's concept of freedom, freedom means belonging to God. One can be free only when one participates in Christ's faithfulness. Likewise, Christians must use freedom responsibly to help others become free. What

do you think about freedom in Galatians (5:1)? How can we read with John 8:31–32: "Then Jesus said to the Jews who had believed in him, 'If you continue in my word, you are truly my disciples; and you will know the truth, and the truth will make you free.'" In John, freedom is the result of following Jesus. That is, freedom has to do with truth. Can you relate truth in Galatians and truth in John? Do they mean the same thing?

Then in Gal 5:3, Paul repeats worriedly: "Once again I testify to every man who lets himself be circumcised that he is obliged to obey the entire law." He is concerned that the Galatians will then be obligated to obey the entire law. Why? For circumcision would arguably amount to conversion to Judaism and would thus place one under an obligation to obey all the law. In other words, he is concerned about the Jewish way or the law-centered religiosity at the cost of faith and Christ. So he repeats his point made many times before: "You who want to be justified by the law have cut yourselves off from Christ; you have fallen away from grace" (Gal 5:4). This verse refers to what he discussed before in Gal 3:6–29 where he vehemently argued that God's blessing of Abraham comes through the faith of Jesus and it is given to those who have faith. God's blessing is therefore by the grace of Jesus and the love of God (cf. Gal 1:6; 2:20).

In the end, those who live by faith through the Spirit will be the righteous ones, as Paul says in Gal 5:5: "For through the Spirit, by faith, we eagerly wait for the hope of righteousness." Here, "the hope of righteousness" means the future righteousness. So Paul expects a time of consummation when they will be all glorified. Until then, he implies that they have to live by faith through the Spirit. In other words, what really matters is "faith working through love," which is the way of Christ (Gal 5:6). So Paul wants to live by Christ's faith, as he says in Gal 2:20: "and it is no longer I who live, but it is Christ who lives in me. And the life I now live in the flesh *I live by the faith of the Son of God, who loved me and gave himself for me*" (italics for emphasis). If people live by faith, following Christ, neither circumcision nor uncircumcision counts for anything (Gal 5:6). So "in Christ Jesus" in Gal 5:6 is a modal dative that points to the manner or the way of Christ.

In Gal 5:7–12, Paul cautions the Galatians to ward off those who prevented them "from obeying the truth" because "the truth of the gospel" may be compromised (cf. Gal 2:5, 14). Here, the truth has to do with God's gospel or his power for salvation to everyone who has faith. The gospel is not restrained or controlled by any culture or the law. So earlier in Gal 2:5, Paul says: "we did not submit to them even for a moment, so that the truth of the gospel might always remain with you." Similarly, he also says in Gal 2:14: "But when I saw that they were not acting consistently with the truth of the gospel, I said to Cephas before them all, 'If you, though a Jew, live like a gentile and not like a Jew, how can you compel the gentiles to live like Jews?'" Those who prevented the Galatians from obeying the truth are mentioned in Gal 1:6–7: "I am astonished that you are so quickly deserting the one who called you in the grace of Christ and are turning to a different gospel—not that there is another gospel, but there are some who are confusing you and want to pervert the gospel of Christ." Those who confuse them and want to pervert the gospel of Christ do not follow the truth of the gospel, which is the power of the God of salvation for both Jews *and gentiles*. This gospel needs faith, not law-centered religion.

Paul is very concerned about the health of the whole community, as he says: "A little yeast leavens the whole batch of dough" (Gal 5:9). He even says: "But whoever it is that is confusing you will pay the penalty" (Gal 5:10). He also says if he preached circumcision, he would not be persecuted (Gal 5:11). Furthermore, in that case, there would be no offense of the cross, meaning there would be no gospel of Christ crucified (cf. 1 Cor 2:2). He utters a very harsh saying: "I wish those who unsettle you would castrate themselves!" (Gal 5:12). This is a real curse, which cannot be said to persons. Even if he was very upset with the Galatian situation and was so certain about his gospel, this curse is hardly defensible. He actually uttered a similar curse very early on, in Gal 1:8–9: "But even if we or an angel from heaven should proclaim to you a gospel contrary to what we proclaimed to you, let that one be accursed! As we have said before, so now I repeat, if anyone proclaims to you a gospel contrary to what you received, let that one be accursed!" This curse applies to an angel and anyone, including himself, if anyone proclaims another gospel. The curse word is simple though: "let that one be accursed." However, in Gal 5:12, it is too cruel to understand it. Indeed, Paul seems very angry when he also refers to the Galatians as having been "bewitched"!

Galatians 5:13–15 reiterates the point made in Gal 5:1. In Gal 5:13, Paul reminds the Galatians of their responsibility for freedom: "For you were called to freedom, brothers and sisters; only do not use your freedom as an opportunity for self-indulgence, but through love become slaves to one another." Christ's setting them free is not only for them but for others.

They have to serve one another without fighting (Gal 5:15). They were called to freedom, which means their job is to ensure that freedom is enacted in a person, a community, and society. The whole law is summed up in a single commandment and supports this work of freedom for others: "You shall love your neighbor as yourself."[2]

5:16–26 "LIVE BY THE SPIRIT"

16 Live by the Spirit, I say, and do not gratify the desires of the flesh. 17 For what the flesh desires is opposed to the Spirit, and what the Spirit desires is opposed to the flesh; for these are opposed to each other, to prevent you from doing what you want. 18 But if you are led by the Spirit, you are not under the law. 19 Now the works of the flesh are obvious: fornication, impurity, licentiousness, 20 idolatry, sorcery, enmities, strife, jealousy, anger, quarrels, dissensions, factions, 21 envy, drunkenness, carousing, and things like these. I am warning you, as I warned you before: those who do such things will not inherit the kingdom of God. 22 By contrast, the fruit of the Spirit is love, joy, peace, patience, kindness, generosity, faithfulness, 23 gentleness, and self-control. There is no law against such things. 24 And those who belong to Christ Jesus have crucified the flesh with its passions and desires. 25 If we live by the Spirit, let us also be guided by the Spirit. 26 Let us not become conceited, competing against one another, envying one another.

Paul's charge to the Galatians continues with another mandate of the gospel: "Live by the Spirit, I say, and do not gratify the desires of the flesh" (Gal 6:16). This mandate is also evident in Rom 8:5–9:

5 For those who live according to the flesh set their minds on the things of the flesh, but those who live according to the Spirit set their minds on the things of the Spirit. 6 To set the mind on the flesh is death, but to set the mind on the Spirit is life and peace. 7 For this reason the mind that is set on the flesh is hostile to God; it does not submit to God's law—indeed it cannot, 8 and those who are in the flesh cannot please God. 9 But you are not in the flesh; you are in the Spirit, since the Spirit of God dwells in you. Anyone who does not have the Spirit of Christ does not belong to him.

---

2. If there is a true love of neighbor, there is also a true love of God. So, Paul does not need to say the whole law is summed up with the love of God and the love of neighbor.

"Live by the Spirit" means to be guided by the Spirit, which means one should not gratify the desires of the flesh. This sounds like Rom 8:13: "By the Spirit put to death the deeds of the body." "Flesh" (*sarx*) in Gal 6:16 and "the body" (*soma*) in Rom 8:13 are interchangeable; the point is Christians have to live by the Spirit, not by their sinful passions. Paul is not a dualist in the sense that the body or the flesh is evil and that only the spirit is pure and immortal. While the flesh is weak, he believes it can be overcome by the Spirit. That overcoming is possible when one puts to death the deeds of the body (or the desires of the flesh) by the Spirit. He also says there is opposition between what the flesh desires and what the Spirit desires. The former is listed in Gal 5:19–21 and the latter is in Gal 5:22–23. In order to get the fruit of the Spirit, the Galatians have to be led by the Spirit. If they are led by the Spirit, they are not under the law (Gal 5:18). Here, "being not under the law" does not mean they are free from the law, but it states the status of Christians who overcame by the Spirit negative influences of laws, including Jewish laws and Roman customs and laws. In fact, "under law" (*hypo nomon*) appeared earlier in Gal 4:4–5 and 4:21, and we interpreted it not as "under the Torah" but as the condition of control.

By contrast, if they live by the Spirit, the fruits of the Spirit are many: "love, joy, peace, patience, kindness, generosity, faithfulness, gentleness, and self-control" (Gal 5:22–23). Nothing or nobody can block the virtues because they come from the Spirit. But these virtues are not possible unless one crucifies the flesh with its passions and desires, as he says in Gal 5:24: "And those who belong to Christ Jesus have crucified the flesh with its passions and desires." Lastly, he concludes the mandate of the gospel he began in Gal 5:16 and reiterates it in Gal 5:25–26: "If we live by the Spirit, let us also be guided by the Spirit. Let us not become conceited, competing against one another, envying one another."

> **Consider and discuss:** For Paul, Jesus's followers have to live by the Spirit (Gal 6:16). What does it mean to live by the Spirit? Can you compare Gal 6:16 with Rom 8:13? What is the role of the Spirit in Galatians?

6:1–10 "FULFILL THE LAW OF CHRIST"

1 My friends, if anyone is detected in a transgression, you who have received the Spirit should restore such a one in a spirit of gentleness. Take care that you yourselves are not tempted. 2 Bear one another's burdens, and in this way you will fulfill the law of Christ. 3 For if those who are nothing think they are something, they deceive themselves. 4 All must test their own work; then that work, rather than their neighbor's work, will become a cause for pride. 5 For all must carry their own loads. 6 Those who are taught the word must share in all good things with their teacher. 7 Do not be deceived; God is not mocked, for you reap whatever you sow. 8 If you sow to your own flesh, you will reap corruption from the flesh; but if you sow to the Spirit, you will reap eternal life from the Spirit. 9 So let us not grow weary in doing what is right, for we will reap at harvest time, if we do not give up. 10 So then, whenever we have an opportunity, let us work for the good of all, and especially for those of the family of faith.

Paul's mandate of the gospel continues in Gal 6:1–10 with slightly different language: "Fulfill the law of Christ." He emphasizes the need for mutual care and a mind of gentleness in dealing with community situations. Thus he begins: "My friends, if anyone is detected in a transgression, you who have received the Spirit should restore such a one in a spirit of gentleness. Take care that you yourselves are not tempted. Bear one another's burdens, and in this way you will fulfill the law of Christ" (Gal 6:1–2). Here a person involved in a transgression is not advised to be cast out or cursed. Paul's advice here is contrasted with the early situations where he cursed those who confused the Galatians about the gospel. The issue here maybe involves a minor violation of ethical codes or community rules of love and care. A person committing a transgression needs an opportunity to repent and to be restored to the community in a spirit of gentleness, which is the fruit of the Spirit. The spiritual person does not rule over others or judge them. So the community as a whole needs to follow the work of the Spirit and maintain the Spirit-led community of love and care. At the same time, Paul warns that believers must check themselves so that they may not be tempted.

He also asks the Galatians "to bear one another's burdens, and in this way you will fulfill the law of Christ." Here "the law of Christ" sounds interesting because many times in this letter Paul has contrasted Christ or faith with the law or works of the law. Now he applies the same Greek word (*nomos*) to Christ, implying another meaning of the law, which is a law or a rule. So the law of Christ is none other than the principle or the way of Christ. That is, what Christ did and how he behaved constitutes his law. Christ gave his life to set the Galatians free from the present evil age (Gal 1:4). Therefore, they must follow the way of Christ, caring for one another, checking who they are before God, and how vulnerable they are in their everyday life. So he advises them this way: "For if those who are nothing think they are something, they deceive themselves" (Gal 6:3). I can rephrase this verse as follows: "If those who think they are something without knowing they are nothing, they are really nothing, unqualified for anything." In other words, they have to know they are nothing before God and see the grace of Jesus in his love of them and in his crucifixion. When they realize how small and weak they are, they may depend on the Spirit. Then they can do something for others through the way of Christ. They can stand firm in Christ, live in and to freedom. Therefore, "all must test their own work" (Gal 6:4) and "carry their own loads" on behalf of others and the community. In Gal 6:6–10, Paul continues to advise the Galatians to support one another by sharing what they have with others, sow to the Spirit rather than to the flesh, and not to give up good works in Christ until harvest time.

> **Consider and discuss:** "The law of Christ" seems a conclusion of the letter in the sense that the Galatians must follow Jesus and imitate his faithfulness. What do you think about this and what is your interpretation of "the law of Christ" in Gal 6:1–10? How can you relate to "living by the Spirit" (Gal 5:16–26)? Can you read Gal 6:1–10 with Rom 3:27 ("the law of faith") and Rom 7:22 and 7:25 ("the law of God")?

SECTION VII

6:11–18

The Letter's Conclusion

11 See what large letters I make when I am writing in my own hand! 12 It is those who want to make a good showing in the flesh that try to compel you to be circumcised—only that they may not be persecuted for the cross of Christ. 13 Even the circumcised do not themselves obey the law, but they want you to be circumcised so that they may boast about your flesh. 14 May I never boast of anything except the cross of our Lord Jesus Christ, by which the world has been crucified to me, and I to the world. 15 For neither circumcision nor uncircumcision is anything; but a new creation is everything! 16 As for those who will follow this rule—peace be upon them, and mercy, and upon the Israel of God. 17 From now on, let no one make trouble for me; for I carry the marks of Jesus branded on my body. 18 May the grace of our Lord Jesus Christ be with your spirit, brothers and sisters. Amen.

WE HAVE COME TO the last section of the commentary, Gal 6:11–18, The Letter's Conclusion, which includes Paul's greeting and his last word/charge to the Galatians. He emphasizes that this is his authentic letter, which carries his presence, and writes: "See what large letters I make when I am writing in my own hand!" (Gal 6:11). Then, in Gal 6:12, he again warns against the circumcision faction, saying: "It is those who want to make a good showing in the flesh that try to compel you to be circumcised—only that they may not be persecuted for the cross of Christ." In other words, they boast about their body and compel others to be circumcised like them. In the end, the common ground for them is the circumcision about which they feel comfortable and boastful. In this way, they can avoid persecution by other Jews because they stay in the Jewish way and culture, not following the message of the cross of Christ. But Paul says they do not obey the law, which means the law is not interpreted well and practiced with a focus on the love of neighbor. The law is not the first thing to keep but the second thing, after faith. That is, while the law is holy, it cannot replace faith or God's promise. Faithfulness to God must inform the law. What really matters is not the law itself but faith working through love (Gal 5:6). The law is fulfilled through love and faith, and Jesus did it. But those in the circumcision faction do not care about the law's purpose; rather, they use it to control others and their bodies through circumcision (Gal 6:13).

But Paul says he will not "boast of anything except the cross of our Lord Jesus Christ, by which the world has been crucified to me, and I to the world" (Gal 6:14). This verse refers to Gal 2:19–20: "For through the law I died to the law, so that I might live to God. I have been crucified with Christ; and it is no longer I who live, but it is Christ who lives in me. And the life I now live in the flesh I live by faith in the Son of God, who loved me and gave himself for me." Galatians 6:14 can be properly understood alongside Gal 2:19–20. For Paul, the cross of Jesus shows his costly love of people and the world. In other words, his work of God to bring justice and freedom to the world made him be crucified because the world hated him. Here, the world represents evil powers, people, and authorities. God raised him from the dead and judged the world. Through Christ's love and his grace, the world began to be hopeful because people would repent and come back to God. So Paul confesses that through the cross of Christ the world has been crucified to him, and he to the world. This means for him the world has been judged by God and defeated by Christ through his love of it. The world can be a new, redeemable place through Christ's cross. He has been crucified to the world in the sense that he will follow the way of Christ to redeem the world. He died with Christ to do this task of freedom for the world (cf. Gal 1:4).

Then in Gal 6:15, he briefly introduces the idea of a new creation, which is a prevalent theme in Romans and 2 Corinthians. Here, he does not explore this theme very much because he has to finish the letter. But his point is, as he said earlier in Gal 5:6, "neither circumcision nor uncircumcision is anything" (Gal 6:15) because what really matters is "faith working through love" (Gal 5:6).

In Gal 6:16–18, Paul says his greetings and even here he inserts his advice or charge to the Galatians. First, "those who will follow this rule" are given the greeting of peace and mercy (Gal 6:16). "This rule" is the guidance of the Spirit or the law of Christ. But one of the issues in Gal 6:16 concerns the phrase "upon the Israel of God." Who is Israel here? Perhaps he means Jews in general or the whole Israel, as he does when he deals with the place of Israel in Rom 9–11. For example, he hopes that all Israel will be saved (Rom 11:26). Second, in Gal 6:17, he repeats his theology and ethics about Christ, which is also an important part of the gospel of Christ: "From now on, let no one make trouble for me; for I carry the marks of Jesus branded on my body" (cf. Gal 2:20; 6:14). Then, Paul's real last greeting comes in Gal 6:18: "May the grace of our Lord Jesus Christ be with your spirit, brothers and sisters. Amen."

> **Consider and discuss:** In Gal 6:14, Paul says he will not "boast of anything except the cross of our Lord Jesus Christ, by which the world has been crucified to me, and I to the world." Why is the cross so crucial to Paul's theology and what message of the cross does he emphasize on to the Galatians? Then, in Gal 6:15, he mentions a new creation. What does the cross have to do with a new creation?

Bibliography

Badiou, Alain. *St. Paul: The Foundation of Universalism*. Stanford, CA: Stanford University Press, 2003.

Barclay, John. *Obeying the Truth: Paul's Ethics in Galatia*. Edinburgh: T. & T. Clark, 1988.

———. *Paul and the Gift*. Grand Rapids: Eerdmans, 2017.

Berchman, Robert. "Galatians (1:1–5): Paul and Greco-Roman Rhetoric." In *The Galatians Debate*, edited by Mark D. Nanos, 60–72. Peabody, MA: Hendrickson, 2002.

Betz, Hans. *Galatians*. Philadelphia: Fortress, 1979.

———. "The Literary Composition and Function of Paul's Letter to the Galatians." In *The Galatians Debate*, edited by Mark D. Nanos, 3–28. Peabody, MA: Hendrickson, 2002.

Byrne, Brendan. *Galatians and Romans*. Collegeville, MN: Liturgical, 2010.

Cosgrove, Charles. *The Cross and the Spirit: A Study in the Argument and Theology of Galatians*. Macon, GA: Mercer University Press, 1988.

Dunn, James D. G. *The Epistle to the Galatians*. Peabody, MA: Hendrickson, 1993.

———. "The Incident at Antioch (Gal 2:11–18)." *Journal for the Study of the New Testament* 5 (1983) 3–57.

Eastman, Susan. *Recovering Paul's Mother Tongue: Language and Theology in Galatians*. Minneapolis, MN: Fortress, 2007.

Eisenbaum, Pamela. *Paul Was Not a Christian: The Original Message of a Misunderstood Apostle*. New York: HarperOne, 2010.

Fee, Gordon. *God's Empowering Presence: The Holy Spirit in the Letters of Paul*. Peabody, MA: Hendrickson, 1994.

Fredriksen, Paula. *Paul: The Pagans' Apostle*. New Haven, CT: Yale University Press, 2017.

———. "Why Should a 'Law-Free' Mission Mean a 'Law-Free' Apostle?" *Journal of Biblical Literature* 134.3 (2015) 637–50.

Gager, John. *Reinventing Paul*. New York: Oxford University Press, 2000.

Hall, Robert. "The Rhetorical Outline for Galatians." In *The Galatians Debate*, edited by Mark D. Nanos, 29–38. Peabody, MA: Hendrickson, 2002.

Hays, Richard. *The Faith of Jesus Christ: The Narrative Substructure of Galatians 3:1—4:11*. Grand Rapids: Eerdmans, 2001.

Hübner, Hans. *Law in Paul's Thought: A Contribution to the Development of Pauline Theology*. Edinburg: T. & T. Clark, 1984.

Keener, Craig. *Galatians*. Cambridge: Cambridge University Press, 2018.

———. *Galatians: A Commentary*. Grand Rapids: Baker Academic, 2019.

Kim, Yung Suk. "Between Text and Sermon: Hebrews 11:8–16." *Interpretation: A Journal of Bible and Theology* 72.2 (2018) 204–6.

———— *Messiah in Weakness: A New Portrait of Jesus from the Perspective of the Dispossessed*. Eugene, OR: Cascade, 2016.

————. *Preaching the New Testament Again: Faith, Freedom, and Transformation*. Eugene, OR: Cascade, 2019.

————. *Rereading Romans from the Perspective of Paul's Gospel: A Literary and Theological Commentary*. Eugene, OR: Resource, 2019.

————. *A Theological Introduction to Paul's Letters: Exploring a Threefold Theology of Paul*. Eugene, OR: Cascade, 2011.

————. Review of Pamela Eisenbaum, *Paul Was Not a Christian: The Original Message of a Misunderstood Apostle*. New York: HarperOne, 2009. *Review of Biblical Literature* 2010.

Longenecker, Richard. *Galatians*. Waco, TX: Word, 1990.

Longenecker, Bruce. *The Triumph of Abraham's God: The Transformation of Identity in Galatians*. Nashville, TN: Abingdon, 1998.

Martyn, J. Louis. *Galatians*. New York: Doubleday, 1997.

————. "A Law-observant Messiah to the Gentiles." *Scottish Journal of Theology* 38 (1985) 307–24.

Matera, Frank. *Galatians*. Collegeville, MN: Liturgical, 1992.

Metzger, Bruce M. *A Textual Commentary on the Greek New Testament*. Stuttgart, Germany: United Bible Societies, 1971.

Nanos, Mark D. *The Irony of Galatians: Paul's Letter in First-Century Context*. Minneapolis, MN: Fortress, 2002.

Roetzel, Calvin. *The Letters of Paul: Conversations in Context*. Louisville, KY: WJKP, 1998.

Sanders, E. P. *Paul and Palestinian Judaism*. Philadelphia: Fortress, 1977.

————. *Paul, the Law, and the Jewish People*. Minneapolis: Fortress, 1983.

Smit, Joop. "The Letter of Paul to the Galatians: A Deliberative Speech." In *The Galatians Debate*, edited by Mark D. Nanos, 39–59. Peabody, MA: Hendrickson, 2002.

Smith, Mitzi J., and Yung Suk Kim. *Toward Decentering the New Testament: A Reintroduction*. Eugene, OR: Cascade, 2018.

Thielman, Frank. *From Plight to Solution: A Jewish Framework for Understanding Paul's View of the Law in Galatians and Romans*. Leiden: Brill, 1989.

Warrior, Robert. "Canaanites, Cowboys, and Indians: Deliverance, Conquest, and Liberation Theology Today." Accessed, 5/26/2019. https://www.rmselca.org/sites/rmselca.org/files/media/canaanites_cowboys_and_indians.pdf.

www.ingramcontent.com/pod-product-compliance
Lightning Source LLC
Chambersburg PA
CBHW020210090426

42734CB00008B/1004